Mike Nicol

Sea-Mountain, Fire City

Living in Cape Town

KWELA BOOKS

Some of the material included in this book first appeared
in articles in *Business Day*, *Cape Times*, *Mail & Guardian*, *The
Sunday Times*, *Out There,* and *Wespennest*, Austria.

Engraving on the cover entitled "Darling Street"
by Katherine Bull
Cover and book design by Nazli Jacobs
Set in Stone
Printed and bound by NBD
Drukkery Street, Goodwood, Western Cape
First edition, first printing 2001

ISBN 0-7957-0098-9

Contents

Preface: Imagining Cape Town

In 1997 I spent a year in Berlin that was deeply unsettling. I couldn't adjust to the urban density of a city where the only 'hills' were the eight man-made rubble mounds such as Teufelsberg (devil's mountain) or those at Volkspark Friedrichshain that were piled up when the city was rebuilt at the end of World War Two. I was a stranger out of my element. So often the sky was low and heavy and I felt hemmed in, trapped by a grey claustrophobia. I wanted light and air and space. In a somewhat desperate attempt to acclimatise I wandered around the city trying to make it familiar, trying to find its secret life. By that I mean the sense that made Berlin Berlin.

It was, I decided, a spectacularly ugly city. I was also told, by Berliners and non-Berliners alike, that it was tough, brusque and in-your-face. Berlin doesn't care, was the general consensus.

In my efforts to come to terms with this city and the way it was described I thought often of Cape Town – the city where I was born, spent much of my childhood and the last twenty years. As Berliners were quick to give their city a personality, so I started giving Cape Town human characteristics. I would catch myself saying things like 'the heart of Cape Town', 'the face of Cape Town', or referring to Cape Town as 'she' – 'she's a wonderful city to live in, but she can be a bitch sometimes.' This 'she' had emotions (she could be moody and difficult) and characteristics (fair, even beautiful), with wants (a desire for flamboyance) and needs (a care and attention that was heart-wrenching). Part of this was my attempting to find a sense of place, now that I was (temporarily, admittedly) displaced. Of course the irony that this search should begin in an ugly city when my own was so alluring wasn't wasted. Perhaps if the other city had been Prague or Paris everything might have worked out differently; I like to think that only Berlin could have influenced the way this story would be told.

For one thing Berlin – like my version of Cape Town – was a city where history was written on every stone, often literally in bullet marks from World War Two firefights, but more usually in the accumulated age of old buildings that had stood through extraordinary times. The secret life of Berlin, I discovered, was its political power: this had led to foreign invasions and occupations, let alone internal turmoil which had manifested at various times in riots and assassinations. The city had a grim and unhappy history, and often on my walks I wondered how much of this had soaked into the lives of today's Berliners. In fact whenever I came up against their rudeness I ascribed it to the city.

At the end of 1997, now thoroughly restive, I returned to Cape Town, to the city that once I had been accused of dismissing with indifference. 'Some of the city's writers just happen to live here,' ran the criticism, 'this place is of little or no interest to them as a subject for their writing.' Then I was singled out for having noted on the jacket of a novel that I lived 'on a wind-blown peninsula in the South Atlantic' and not 'in Cape Town'.

The biographical blurb was tongue in cheek but as I tried to regain my old way of life I began to think my critic had a point. Although I had always written the city into my fiction, perhaps I hadn't been living in Cape Town. Perhaps I had yet to understand the meaning of that phrase: a sense of place. I remembered the poet, Stephen Watson's, argument that writers needed to make Cape Town 'a place in the mind' for if they didn't 'not even its inhabitants [could] live there imaginatively'. After the richness of Berlin that existed as much by the immediacy of its fictional characters and their imagined stories as by its reality, I understood what he was getting at. And as Cape Town was South Africa's oldest city, something would be seriously wrong if there were no literature to give it a resonance beyond the spectacle of Table Mountain, the Waterfront, and the wild and windy heights of Cape Point. Without stories and poetic imagery, how could the city lay claim to the status? History wasn't enough, it had to be reimagined. So I started to look at Cape Town the way Berlin had taught me to read a city.

After three and a half centuries Cape Town as a site of memory is thick with tales and plots, although perhaps the tour guides have been quicker to capitalise on this than the writers. Daily in Church

Square you can hear the couriers conjuring up the middle of the eighteenth century to groups of Germans, Dutch, Americans, and Japanese. They point to two of the city's first buildings – the Groote Kerk and directly opposite it the Slave Lodge, a unique institution where the Dutch East India Company kept its slaves – and evoke the city that is layered behind the one we see. They stand on the traffic island on which the 'slave tree' grew and under which slaves were auctioned, and those lives are made real again. They mention that at night in the mid-nineteenth century, after curfew, Church Square was deserted, scavenged by packs of dogs and even by hyenas.

The tourists look around and see a modern city at work. They are not far from Parliament, where the second popularly elected government is in power. Overhead the sky is deep blue, behind the office blocks Table Mountain looms through the salt haze. The cry of seagulls can be heard above the traffic. But, of course, beneath what can be seen the secret life continues.

The difficulty with imagining Cape Town is that it has never had one reality: from the start there were the Khoi, the Dutch company officials, and the slaves. They all gave different meanings to the growing town, and ever since the versions of Cape Town have multiplied.

As a port Cape Town has always taken in groups of people, but inevitably grudgingly, and always by insisting they assimilate into, rather than try to take over, the city. This grouchiness is part of the city's secret life, a defence because it is open to the world, and desirable. After all it is the sea that gave the Dutch East India Company access to the tip of a continent that even today is difficult to traverse overland, just as it was earth – cultivatable ground – that brought them ashore. Unsurprisingly, Cape Town's first metaphor was one of succour as the Dutch East India Company's refreshment station provided fresh victuals for the ships sailing between Holland and the Company's dominions in Malaysia. Simultaneously, however, the metaphor of succour was rendered harshly ironic as the Khoi were dispossessed of their summer pasturage, and slaves were brought to service a settlement that must have represented suffering and unhappiness to them.

And then there is the summer wind – a trade wind, rather bleakly called the southeaster – that is indisputably another of Cape Town's shaping characteristics. Each year, from October to March, for weeks on end the wind rattles across the city covering every surface in a fine grit, fraying people's nerves until, like the city's oak leaves late in the season, they are brittle and cracked and burnt. After a long blow there is a tension to the city visible in the grimaces on people's faces as they push down Adderley Street against the wind.

Despite this unease, the wind is also called the Cape Doctor. Not because it carries medicinal properties but because in previous centuries it blew away the stench of sewage and rot that made the old town unbearable and was one of the reasons the middle classes moved out and over the ridge to Rondebosch and Wynberg. Today again, the southeaster is a doctor. When it doesn't blow the city is blanketed by a brown haze – a concoction of chemical emissions, diesel and petrol fumes, and smoke from the fires of the ever-growing number of people who don't have electricity – that could soon render Cape Town's air as noxious as that of Mexico City, Los Angeles, Athens, or Tokyo.

But the most significant element in Cape Town's secret life is fire. Increasingly I began to realise that fire was not only Cape Town's dominant form of protest, but a persistent crackle at the edge of our lives. For one thing the squatter communities live with the constant threat of fires that all too frequently sweep through the settlements, burning shacks, causing death and mutilation. For another Cape Town's mountains blaze most years, each time reminding us of a characteristic buried deeply in the nature of the city.

For two weeks in January 2000 an inferno raged across the southern peninsula. Some houses were razed but a good many more were saved thanks to the tireless efforts of the regular firefighters and scores of volunteers. Many of the firefighters came from parts of the city that were not threatened by fire: parts like Athlone, Mitchells Plain, Manenberg, Rylands Estate, Lavender Hill. In other words many of the firefighters were coloured. Mostly the houses they sought to save were owned by whites.

Once it was a commonly held truth among whites that the fires were started by coloureds because, in those days, the fire services paid people who came to help them beat out the flames. In January 2000 it was a commonly held truth among whites that the fires were started by arsonists. It was never said, it didn't have to be, but by arsonists those who held this truth meant coloureds.

Fire has a particular history in Cape Town. In the town's early years under the Dutch East India Company, and later the British, accidental fires could cause vast damage, especially in times of high wind, as did the Great Fire of 1798, which wiped out cavalry stables, warehouses, private homes, and threatened the jail and customs house. Although an inquiry found that the cause was accidental most whites believed it had been set by runaway slaves. Even at that time their belief was founded on a long tradition.

From the settlement's beginning, many fires had been deliberately started. The Khoi used it as a form of retribution against the invaders, slaves resorted to arson as one of the few expressions of rebellion open to them. In fact the intention of the first slave revolt in 1688 was to burn the town. Three centuries later, during the turmoil of the 1980s, fire was again a dominant feature. Cars were set alight, barricades of burning tyres were thrown across roads, shack settlements were torched by the pro-government wit doeke, suspected traitors were necklaced to a flaming death gruesomely reminiscent of the way convicted arsonists once had been 'roasted' to death by the Company. Since then the fires of destruction have come to express themselves as bomb explosions, and more generally as symbols of violence.

From the beginning Cape Town was built on an accumulation of paradox and contrast: to every development a shadow side. The heart of the city formed below the mountain, yet even as the mountain gave the town its distinctive beauty it also gave the town's slaves a passage to freedom. And when the white citizens saw the night fires of escaped slaves flickering above the town they surely must have recognised a threat.

Almost from its founding people wanted to move away from the settlement to farm or search for freedom, or later to dig diamonds and gold, but Cape Town remained, and with Parliament still sited here, precariously remains, the seat of authority. Nor did the settlement, the town, the city, ever close itself off from the land that lay beyond the distant Hottentots Holland mountains. Unlike many

European towns, or the Dutch East India Company's heavily fortified citadel of Batavia, Cape Town was never barricaded by town walls. Commander Jan van Riebeeck may have planted an almond hedge and erected palisades in an attempt to separate his settlement from the wild interior, but a hedge is only a gesture towards segregation.

Yet its relationship with the forming country and the new cities that grew unashamedly from money was that of the 'Mother': always nurturing, always reaching out, always correcting, always casting a long shadow across the veld.

Unfortunately this beautiful Mother was also, and always had been, corrupt: to modern sensibilities she is built on shame. If the story I would be told by Irefaan Rakiep – a descendant of an Indonesian prince – was part of the shame, so is the violence expressed in gang wars and in gang rapes, in alcoholism and family abuse. As I went searching for a sense of place, Cape Town seemed increasingly to be a city in trauma.

In Berlin I came to appreciate the significant bond between the people and the city: they mirrored one another. There was as much to be learnt from walking on the Unter den Linden as from listening to a friend tell how on the death of her father she discovered that he had never resigned from the Nazi party.

I was also intrigued by Berlin's attempt to reinvent itself on Potsdamer Platz. Where once the Wall had rendered this part of the city a stark image of the Cold War, in 1997 Berlin boasted that the once dead land was now the biggest building site in Europe, if not the world. Hubris was no stranger to the Berlin soul. Then again, there are few more persuasive metaphors than that of building, as I was to discover.

Back in Cape Town what I regarded as my Berlin syndrome – a persistent unease – refused to wear off and I was forced to reassess my place in the city. In many ways, and for many people, life had never been better here: the pavement cafés, the coffee and croissants, the fine restaurants, the jazz, all told of an enticing city. Yet in the shadow-city life was as tough as it had ever been. I looked at the mountain and knew that Cape Town's was a dangerous beauty and that sometimes the city truly terrified me. But then I had heard committed Berliners say much the same about their city, a city where for all my restiveness I'd never felt afraid.

Centuries ago the Portuguese described this spit of land that extends stubbornly into the Atlantic Ocean as the Cape of Storms and the Cape of Plagues. The Dutch changed this to the Cape of Good Hope – of course they had to, they were going to establish a settlement. In that simple act of renaming, the fate of the future city was determined on a principle of contrast and paradox: it would be a city of trouble; it would be a city of hope. It would be a city of beauty; it would be a city crippled by disease. Like many, I was seduced by the attractions and opposites of this city, just as I was fascinated by its story.

1: 'Sometimes There Are Sunny Days In Berlin'

My unwitting search for a place in Cape Town began on a dark Monday evening early in January 1997 as I stepped off a train on to Platform One at Berlin's Bahnhof Zoo. The temperature was below freezing.

We had spent Christmas with friends in Munich and then taken the sleek silver, intercity express to Berlin. Except that for two weeks Germany had been covered by snow so the fast intercity became a stopping train, and one of those stops lasted for three hours – which meant we were going to be very late. Would anyone be at the station to meet us? If they weren't what would we do? Would we find a hotel without too much trouble? I joined the queue at an on-train telephone but when I finally got a chance to call, the contact number just rang. I was going to Berlin to take up a year-long grant from the Deutscher Akademischer Austauschdienst – the DAAD – but this didn't look as if it were shaping up for an auspicious start.

On that Monday night in January, Bahnhof Zoo was doubling as an informal bar, a shelter for the indigent, a main-line drug venue, and a lunatic asylum. As the year progressed I came to understand that this was anyhow a major part of the station's function. In winter the homeless were specifically invited in out of the cold. And as part of a new government policy (I later discovered) attempting to rehabilitate the mildly insane, a number of mad people had been released recently to roam the platforms.

As we innocently left the train looking like Russian émigrés in brightly coloured duvet coats (thrust on us by the Munich friends) I thought we were entering an ice-age apocalypse. A couple on a bench prepared a syringe. Bearded individuals in stained coats glared at us. Suddenly a man rushed out of the crowd and started talking to Jill and making signs that she should follow him urgently. He tugged at her padded sleeve, spit spraying from his mouth as he seemed to berate her. She recoiled from the onslaught and shook free her arm. He gabbled at her furiously, then burst into tears. We pushed quickly past him, anxiously glancing up and down the platform for the

15

man from the DAAD. Surely they could not have deserted us? Surely they must have worked out what train we were on? After all they had faxes giving train numbers and arrival times.

I had expected to be met by someone who could escort us through the medieval hordes to a climatically controlled Mercedes Benz that would glide through the city's white streets to the warm and cosy apartment that must surely await us. Soon, ensconced in comfortable armchairs, we would uncork a Bordeaux red and toast our arrival in the city that had been so much a part of our dreams for the past year.

No, we were on our own. Except for the insistent little man who was again tugging at Jill's sleeve. We tried to pretend he didn't exist, that he was merely a figment escaped from a nightmare and of no substance. We tried to talk through a plan of action, but he was shouting so loudly we could hardly hear ourselves. We had three suitcases, shoulder bags, a laptop, and felt as clumsy as Michelin men. What to do? Where to go? The man pulled at us, tried to take the luggage. Could he be the man from the DAAD? The thought was as fleeting as it was ludicrous. Some doors opened before us and we charged into a lift. The little man stayed on the platform, begging us to come back. His face became infinitely sad.

'Come out. Come out,' he pleaded. He could not have looked more mournful were he watching his beloved family descend to hell.

The lift doors closed and he was gone. I pushed a button with an icon that could either have represented a plate, knife and fork or a skull and crossbones. The lift went down a floor and the doors opened on a beaming Italian waiter inviting us into his trattoria. We followed him gratefully, and ordered beer and tortellini. I then made some phone calls. And in less time than it took to get indigestion from the tortellini, the man from the DAAD was approaching our table.

'Tzo,' he said superciliously, 'you should have come by Lufthansa, this would have been a much better arrangement. Then there would not be such a confusion.'

Soon we were in his Mercedes, an early seventies model that was not climatically controlled but certainly heated to a stifling degree for anyone wearing a duvet coat. He drove up the snowed Kurfürstendamm, pointing out designer boutiques and cinemas and CD megastores and clubs, theatres, restaurants, and recited the numbers of the buses on this route. At the top of the boulevard he swung dramatically left across the traffic into a street called Storkwinkel.

'Here is your address,' he said, ramping the curb and stopping in someone's entrance. 'Ja, I won't be long so this is alright.'

We got out and retrieved the bags from the boot.

'That is your balcony,' he said, indicating the first floor where some frozen plants fringed a tiny balcony. 'In summer you can sit out there to eat.' He laughed. 'Doch! Sometimes there are sunny days in Berlin.'

The apartment was spacious and stark, more student squat than middle-class comfort. The walls were cream-coloured, bare, and badly in need of painting. Cobwebs drifted in the high corners and the cornices were shaded with grey dust. A path led across the carpet in the entrance hall like an animal trail through the veld. We entered, somewhat awed by a feeling of emptiness. In the bedroom were two single beds with sagging mattresses and a wardrobe. In the 'lounge/dining room' a round table, four slatted wooden chairs, a small rocking chair for dwarfs, two wire chairs that were as comfortable as sitting on a fence, and an old television set. In the 'study' a glass-topped table, a desk with a severe typist's chair, some bookcases (empty), and a potted plant that was dying of dehydration. The kitchen had another round table and rickety wooden chairs, and a washing machine that operated on one programme only. In the bathroom was an old toilet so throne-like that Jill's feet didn't reach the floor. But of more concern was its large inspection pan. Perhaps to the natives there was much satisfaction to be gained from gazing at a steamy stool, but the subtleties were wasted on us. Nor could I appreciate the stench. Such toilets were not designed for reading on. Never before had I considered what a high point of civilisation the water-filled toilet pan represented.

The DAAD man rushed around ticking off a verbal inventory.

'Tzo,' he said, pausing for breath, 'if there is anything extra here is my telephone number. Tschüs! Auf Wiedersehen.' And he was gone.

Jill stared at the kitchen. 'I'd hoped it might be Miele,' she said wistfully.

During the rest of a dark January and into an equally dark February we more or less worked out the bus, S-Bahn and U-Bahn systems, and become adept at buying bread and cheese from the fearsome shop assistant at nearby Kaisers superette, which also stocked a good number of French and Italian wines. But despite this I wasn't settling easily into the city. I was restless. I felt nothing was happening, that I had been consigned to limbo. The cold militated against exploration, so Berlin remained a vast and dauntingly unknown presence.

We started German lessons with a thoughtful man called Thomas. These became a weekly ritual that began with coffee, went on to a dissection of the German soul, and ended with some hurried attention to the mounds of reading exercises he'd considerately photostatted for us. Then 'Tschüs,' he'd say, flying down the stairs, 'bis Montag Nachmittag um halb drei.' I still do not know if that means half past two or half past three. Every afternoon for the next week Jill and I would find some excuse not to apply our minds to these carefully selected fables. I felt as if I were back in junior school, and rebelled at having to do homework.

Without Thomas we had no way of judging if we were still alive. For we knew no one else, and, reluctant to go through the ritual of putting on coats, gloves, scarves, went nowhere. Nor did the telephone ever ring, and in an age where the significance of a life is measured by the number of telephone calls received each day, I began to wonder if we hadn't passed into a parallel universe. But more to the point: I hated living one floor up in the air. I hated living in a city, and it came as a surprise to realise that all my life had been spent within walking distance of a beach or in suburbs. I hated the low sky, the claustrophobia. I even hated the lack of insects. Most of all I hated the black leafless branches of the tree outside the window.

In fact there came a morning in April when I realised I was shouting at the tree. Screaming for it to leaf. Since January all I'd had were the wet black branches, stark across the window. I wanted sun, endless sky, the far horizon of the ocean. I wanted False Bay. I even considered going home.

Then in May Berlin's trees came into leaf. In a mere ten days spring uncurled a thicket of leaves. I gazed into rich foliage and felt much happier. I couldn't see the street or the apartment blocks opposite. The light in the study was green. There was even a sense of home. The apartment felt completely different. The claustrophobia that had engulfed me in the dark days retreated but never fully disappeared with the longer light. And now that the black branches of the tree outside the window were disguised there was no longer a reminder of my earlier unease.

And Berlin had changed. It was green. It was warm. It was light until ten o'clock at night. There were pavement cafés everywhere. Restaurants put out tables in secret gardens. We unpacked T-shirts and sandals. We rearranged furniture, bought pot plants and planted basil in the window boxes. We opened windows that I'd assumed were stuck closed permanently.

Now that there were insects in the air again – wasps that cruised through the apartment with malicious intent but which could be dispatched using a rolled-up magazine like a baseball bat, and clouds of mosquitoes, midges and fruit flies that, by comparison, made the miasmas of Africa appear healthy – Berlin didn't seem quite so foreign. At least I understood the insect life and the weather, even if there were still more grey than blue to the sky.

But the change in the people came as something of a surprise. Up to the onset of summer I'd come to characterise the Berliner as a sullen, ill-tempered, snappish type. Unnecessarily curt and abrasive, if not downright rude.

Yes, Thomas confirmed laconically. This was an accurate description of his compatriots. Unfortunate but true. Perhaps it had something to do with the nature of Berlin. 'Consider the history,' he would say somewhat enigmatically. 'Berlin is always at the front line. We have been invaded too many times.'

Perhaps he was right. Perhaps this was why all Berlin shop assistants had an ugly propensity to use the word 'Was?' – what? – when they meant 'How may I help you?'

So a badly enunciated, 'Excuse me, could you please help me?' in German, got the response: 'Was?' Obviously it was spoken without a smile, there was frequently no eye contact, and the sound was a clipped, angry hiss: vass?

In twelve months, and despite anticipating it every time I asked for a loaf of bread, postage stamps, Rennies antacids (which for some strange reason could only be purchased from disapproving women in white coats at an Apotheke), I never got used to the abrupt and explosive Was!

Another characteristic of the Berliners was how volubly angry they could get at small transgressions of their city's rules.

Two instances. The first occurred in a bus when I was laden with luggage on the way to the airport. It was mid-morning and the bus crowded with travellers, shoppers, and young mothers with prams. The buses were designed to cater for everyone; seats were set aside for the elderly, there was a luggage area and two demarcated spaces complete with anchor straps reserved for prams. Public transport in Berlin I thought was a dream: efficient, cheap, and safe insofar as the taxi drivers didn't shoot at the bus drivers with AK 47s. But what impressed me particularly was the consideration that had gone into making the buses suitable for use by the encumbered and the frail.

On this morning the bus's luggage area was packed and there was no alternative but for me to stand with the suitcase in the pram space. At some stage a young woman with a pram got on. She assessed the situation, sensibly deciding not to break my ankles in the pursuit of lawfulness. But this wasn't good enough for a woman who turned on me and began shouting at my careless flouting of the rules. I hadn't a clue what she was saying, although she said quite a lot of it. And the more I ignored her the more incensed she became, soliciting support from her compatriots, even appealing to the driver to arbitrate at this gross violation of human rights. The young mother smiled vaguely at me in embarrassment. I shrugged, and examined the woman as she became increasingly apoplectic. Silence in the teeth of anger I have found to be a provocative agent. It drives people to interesting excesses of behaviour, in other words, completely berserk. It can be dangerous however. On one or two occasions when I've jotted down observations in a notebook the situation has come close to life threatening. This incident simply fizzled out and the woman eventually got off in disgust. I was left puzzled but impressed by two things: firstly, the extraordinary number of words that had been brought to bear on the issue and, secondly, by the social conscience that had been summoned to the young mother's assistance. I sensed too that the woman knew I was a stranger – a foreigner, an invader – and that part of her outburst was a defensive xenophobia.

The other incident occurred at Kaisers, the local superette. Like most people I've been shopping in supermarkets all my adult life and never have I spoken to anyone in the check-out queue, let alone been accosted, insulted or shouted at by a fellow queuer. But if it was going to happen sometime somewhere then inevitably Kaisers was going to be the supermarket.

I must mention that Kaisers was remarkable for the quality of its staff. In a year I never got a smile, a good morning, or an Auf Wiedersehen out of them no matter how much I smiled, Guten Morgen'd or tschüs'd. I could only assume they all led unhappy lives in grim apartments.

One afternoon I joined a check-out queue and shuffled patiently to the cashier. Little did I know that behind me a woman was building up a considerable head of vitriol. For long minutes she apparently seethed and boiled as I stacked my few purchases on the conveyor belt. Then her puce face caught my eye. It was all she needed. The pent-up rancour, resentment, and pique at having to wait behind me exploded from her on a harsh breath of yesterday's garlic. I looked at her, completely astonished. The cashier ignored the diatribe, those in the queue behind the demented woman appeared to be doing mental arithmetic. I wondered if I'd been sucked into a lunatic's nightmare. But such was the woman's hostility that I tried to catch words in a desperate effort to understand what rules I'd unwittingly broken. I heard Krankenhaus, hospital, but the rest was just so much German. Whether she was going to the Krankenhaus, or she thought I should go to the Krankenhaus, it was impossible to say. I told her in my best German that I couldn't understand. She went on and on. Hastily I paid the cashier – who still acted as if nothing out of the ordinary was happening – and even more hastily stuffed my groceries into a bag. I fled Kaisers convinced that the most innocuous places in Berlin weren't safe. Perhaps, again, this was a defence against a foreign presence.

Once more Thomas confirmed that, yes, a Berliner could have moments like these. He would cite his theory of a city repeatedly sacked by invading armies and then theorised, somewhat poetically, that maybe it was because Hitler's remains were still entombed in his bunker like radioactive waste. In other words, that in some way Berliners were still contaminated by the Nazi excesses of World War Two. There were times when I wondered about Thomas.

As these incidents, and many other small brushes with the Berliner in the street, had led me to believe that they must be among the most irritable people in the world, their summer behaviour came as a complete surprise.

One of our small daily pleasures was to sit at a pavement café in the early evening, order two large Weissbiers and watch the entertainment. Summer had brought out a host of musicians, mime artists, and pranksters who trawled the pavement cafés at the bottom of the Ku'damm offering entertainment for the price of a few marks dropped into a circulating hat. I found the slapstick and cruel street theatre of the pranksters very satisfying.

One man in particular, who dressed in a shabby grey suit without a tie, received a good stipend from my DAAD grant. The world he created was so nasty that I never grew tired of his tricks. He was a consummate mimic. He would fall into step behind a strolling Berliner and adopt his manner of walking, the slope of his shoulders, even his expressions within moments. The café crowd exploded with laughter, the Berliner looked round, the mimer shadowing his movements undaunted that he'd been caught out. With a tolerant smile and a nod, the Berliner continued his walk. No gesticulating, no shouting, no abuse. Just good-natured humour. The first time I witnessed this gentle acceptance of a fairly savage mocking I choked on my beer.

This particular street artiste's repertoire went further than merely mimicking his victims. I once saw him sidle up to a couple, slip between them and put his arm around the woman. Assuming it was her husband, she let him continue in this familiar way for a good twenty paces before she looked to her side and saw a tramp beaming at her. Again: no hysterical scream, no anger. Merely a smile and a shake of her head as she disengaged herself from him. In his efforts to get some violent reaction to the humiliations he was causing, the mimer resorted to increasingly outrageous measures. He walked behind people and squirted them surreptitiously with water. He blew whistles in their ears. He mussed up their hair. He picked up the hem of a woman's long skirt and pretended he was holding a train. Yet whenever he was caught out, his victims smiled quietly, obviously content in the knowledge that they'd been made to look absolute fools before a café crowd gagging and spluttering with laughter. It all seemed so unlike Berliners. Unless, of course, humiliation – whether dishing it or receiving it – was a central part of the Berlin character?

Early in June home interfered. We received a letter which told that an elderly friend had been found murdered in her Cape Town flat. 'All for a TV set and a VCR.' Literally as I finished reading the letter the telephone rang – a display of synchronicity that would be contrived in fiction yet occurs quite unremarkably in daily life. It was our Muizenberg housesitter.

'You've just become part of the crime statistics,' she said. 'Some kids broke into the house this afternoon.'

'What did they take?' I asked, my mouth gone suddenly dry.

'Oh, you don't have to worry it's all been retrieved,' she explained. 'Someone saw them leaving over the back wall and called the cops. I'm going up to the police station now to collect everything. But it's not that so much, they emptied out every drawer. I don't know what belongs where. The police think they were looking for guns and money. They also hauled out every single saucepan.'

It seemed heartless to be upset by a mere burglary in which everything was recovered within minutes when we had news of another burglary that had ended in murder. Yet we were devastated. Upset beyond reason. Irrationally we blamed Berlin, convinced that if we'd been at home the prowling kids wouldn't have had the opportunity. What next? we lamented.

When I relayed our misfortune to Thomas at our next language lesson he nodded sympathetically and then proceeded to tell tales of Berlin horror and mayhem.

'You see, it is everywhere,' he said finally. 'That is what I tell my nephews and nieces.'

Nevertheless I couldn't be quite as philosophical as Thomas. Restive, and half convinced each time the phone rang that it was to announce another burglary, I felt the need to get out of Berlin for a few days. With the summer warmth, I needed the sea. We decided to take a weekend trip to Rügen Island. But even more important than the break was the sight of Berlin at dawn.

During the whole of 1997 there wasn't a morning to equal this one. Berlin was truly radiant (despite the ranks of building cranes poised over its heart): a huge blue sky, a clarity to the air that shortened the distances. The landmarks were closer, clearer, sharply defined: the sun blazed on the New Synagogue's golden dome and from Golden Ellie on her column above the Grosser Stern. Never before had I noticed how many church steeples made up the skyline, and for an instant I sensed a city far older than the one that had been reconstructed from the rubble of the Second World War. On that bright morning I was given a glimpse of how Berlin could be beautiful, yet there was so much sadness in this moment. And now that the city was being rebuilt once more, and the old heart was being buried yet again, I couldn't imagine in what way this reconstruction would benefit Berlin.

2: *Siamese City*

If in January Berlin had demonstrated the meaning of winter, in August it turned on the heat. Six weeks of humid temperatures upwards of thirty degrees centigrade hung in the city's streets. Never before had I experienced such unrelenting discomfort even in Cape Town during February. It was too hot to work, too hot to sleep. Berlin wilted under general lassitude and dementia. I filled a bath with cold water and periodically during the day, and especially last thing at night, lay submerged until my teeth chattered. The only other refuges were the air-conditioned cinemas but getting to them meant using public transport and public transport meant contact with unacceptable armpits. Cold beer and cold baths, dim rooms and windows open to the merest breeze seemed the best way of handling the oppressive weather.

The natives, however, basked. On the grassy banks around Halensee, the Berliners threw off their clothes and spread their limbs. The sight of so much naked flesh nurtured on beer and Weisswurst – a veal sausage I rather enjoyed despite the skin which had to be peeled off like a used condom and left wilted on the plate – came as something of a shock. I also understood for the first time one of the founding principles of clothing: that as a species we are sexier dressed than undressed. Despite German predilections for health spas and regular bowel movements, let alone the contemporary obsession with gyms, diets, and herbal supplements, I did have to admit a grudging admiration for the many people who clearly didn't give a fig about the shape of their bodies, let alone what others might think of their crinkly hides. I appreciated such in-your-face indifference, even while some of the sights heaved at my digesting Weisswurst. Nevertheless a walk round Halensee proved an interesting introduction to Berlin for our succession of summer guests. Invariably it left them gaping and bemused.

The guests were a welcome distraction, for one thing they brought news of home, for another they brought unprejudiced eyes. Suddenly we were able to see Berlin as tourists saw it: a place where the scars of history may be fascinating and moving but essentially they're someone else's story. Which was the advantage of whistle-stop tours where you didn't have to deal with the history on a day-to-day basis month after month. I thought a lifetime of living in a kind of war had toughened me, it hadn't. Berlin taught me that we developed a thick skin to deal with the country where we lived, but when faced with another's trauma we had no defence.

The first time I visited the city, in June 1989, my host insisted on a quick tour. We had an afternoon free, the sky was clear, the day warm, and I could see he ached to show me his Berlin. I was restless, too, strange cities have an irresistible pull that compels me to walk their streets. And Berlin was a city stranger than most.

In the morning I had flown over the large brown rectangles of GDR agriculture into Berlin's Tegel airport. Given a choice, arriving at the famous Tempelhof like Alec Leamas in John le Carré's *The Spy Who Came In From The Cold* would have been my ideal, but who could quibble about such small matters when Berlin was the destination.

For me the city was then essentially imaginary: a place invented by le Carré. A city of dark streets where the light pooled on wet pavements and occasionally men in trench coats with their collars turned up would step out of the darkness to check their watches. My host's Berlin was not much different, except the sites he showed me were redolent with real events, real tragedies.

We took a taxi to a place on the banks of the River Spree that must have been off Moltkestrasse, not far from the Reichstag. My memory is indistinct but carries images of urban dereliction: cracked concrete paving, grass growing wild, shards of glass. In the canal a patrol boat of armed guards watched us through binoculars. On the lip of the canal wall were some dry wreaths, a bunch of fresh flowers, too. Four months earlier a young man had been shot dead by the border guards as he swam for freedom.

We went next to the lookout platform at Potsdamer Platz. Below was the Wall, brightly graffiti'd on the western side, a dull emptiness on the other. We gazed down on a wide clear run where a few rabbits searched for food. Beyond this, razor wire, barbed wire fences and then the backs of apartments with the windows boarded up. To the left was a tower, the guards watching us through binoculars, for what else was there to distract them in the numbing boredom of this no man's land? In the distance I could see the odd person walking in the grey streets of Mitte but their lives were unimaginable. To the far side was a grassy mound under which were the sealed remains of Hitler's bunker.

We drove next across the city to Hitler's ominous Olympia Stadion where a watchman was cajoled into allowing us in even though the stadium was closed to the public on that afternoon.

The stadium was daunting, heavy, forbidding. My companion ironically referred to it as one of the more restrained examples of Nazi architecture. 'You can just hear them all shouting Sieg Heil,' he said, his tone loaded with repugnance. He was right: the chant seemed to well beneath the silence and I felt that if it found the merest crack the stadium would roar with barely suppressed fury. It was on this track that the black American, Jesse Owens, won four medals in the 1936 Olympics, much to Hitler's obvious annoyance. He refused to congratulate Owens, but contrite Berliners have subsequently named a nearby street after the athlete.

Here, much to our frustration, for we had run out of time, the tour ended, but Berlin had buried a small hook in my skin. Not long afterwards I read Ian McEwan's thriller *The Innocent*, but as wonderfully as he evoked the post-war city, his Berlin was still a cloak and dagger backdrop. What, I wondered, was it really like to live in this divided city? A novel called *The Wall Jumper* by Peter Schneider provided an answer.

After twenty years in West Berlin working as a political journalist, Schneider wrote a funny, spare meditation on the city that had adopted him. He called it the Siamese city and confessed that like most Berliners he didn't see the Wall anymore. A wry confession subverted by an entire book devoted to the concrete and barbed wire surrounding his life.

And then for Schneider and his fellow Berliners the impossible happened, the Wall fell. The euphoria reached across the world and as I listened to radio reports I wondered about the family of the young man shot swimming across the Spree. How did they grieve for him now? Had he waited eight months he could have walked unchecked to the brazen ugly Europa-Center. So often, I thought, history rendered politics a tragic nonsense where the change from one system to another could be reduced to a body count at worst, to a mistake at best.

How other people see cities is always instructive. And my companion's Berlin revealed so hastily on that afternoon in many ways determined my response to the city in 1997. At least I can see that now, at the time I felt there was only one city, and this city was the one I chose to reveal to our summer guests.

As I've always had a secret desire to be a tour guide I put together a Grim Day-Tour of Berlin. There are few things that appeal to me more than hauling up the unsuspecting against the dark side of humankind. The Grim Guide took them down the great Kurfürstendamm boulevard now shaded by plane trees. At the bottom was the Gedächtniskirche, a blackened memorial stump that was all that remained of a six-towered neo-Gothic church built to glorify, in no particular order, God and Kaiser Wilhelm I. The church was reduced to rubble, as was most of Berlin, by two years of Allied bombing raids.

A short distance farther on, at Wittenbergplatz U-Bahn entrance, stood a display board listing the concentration camps.

Next the Grim Guide pointed to some of the architectural starkness: the wastelands of Breitscheidplatz and the gaudy Europa-Center which competed with Alexanderplatz as a hang-out site for bored youth and the bored police who came to mind them. The Europa-Center also went to prove that in the struggle for ugliness, capitalism could match communist concretism every inch of the way.

However, as the bus turned right along the Landwehrkanal, through the trees on the left could be glimpsed the toy-block style of the Bauhaus. This was a building I never tired of. It was stylish, but there was also something humorous and childlike about the lines. Unlike Mies van der Rohe's Neue Nationalgalerie farther down the road. It might be merely a superstructure, a canopied slab, but it sat on acres of black paving and appeared to be nothing more than a huge shelter for pedestrians needing to get out of the rain. Most of the building was underground which seemed to echo a Berlin penchant for bunkers.

When the bus stopped at the bombed ruin of Anhalter Bahnhof the Grim Guide went up Stresemannstrasse, once *the* street of Nazi headquarters, and turned right after the lovely Martin-Gropius Bau, still chipped and scarred by shrapnel and bullets. Here was half a century of history in one confined area. Beyond Gropius Bau was the Topographie des Terrors where excavations were continuing to reveal Nazi torture chambers. Beside this was one of the few remaining sections of the Wall.

From here it was a short walk along Zimmerstrasse to Checkpoint Charlie which, by 1997, had lost all resonance of the Cold War days and the cluster of museums and shops had managed to turn history into kitsch.

The Grim Guide next took the U-Bahn to Französische Strasse for Kaffee und Kuchen at the nearby Café Mohring – the eastern version of the more famous Ku'damm café – or lunch in Borcherds, which showed as many signs of street fighting on its facade as the Martin-Gropius Bau.

The next stop was for me the most evocative corner of Berlin, the old Jewish quarter behind the Hackescher Markt S-Bahn station. In

1997 most of Oranienburger Strasse was lined by sooty buildings that had survived the 1940s bombings but were crumbling from GDR neglect. Here and there restoration work had begun but the area really needed to be retained as one huge memorial. The full meaning of the place only struck when you turned the corner into Grosse Hamburger Strasse. Some fifty metres up the street was the Old Jewish Cemetery – or what was left of it. The cemetery dated back to 1672. In 1943 the Gestapo destroyed it, smashing tombstones and disinterring the remains. The site was levelled and became a collection point from which people were herded to the transports leaving for Auschwitz and Theresienstadt. Some fifty-five thousand Berlin Jews began that enforced and hopeless journey from this cemetery. Now the cemetery was a garden. On the pavement stood a sculpture of a group of emaciated and helpless Jews, their fate clearly etched in their faces. At their feet, those who chose not to forget left small stones in memoriam.

From here the route was by tram to Volkspark Friedrichshain. There were two reasons for this excursion. The first was of architectural significance because on the corner of Karl-Marx-Allee and Otto-Braun-Strasse was a condemned block of flats that in its size and structure contained all the nightmares of the high density urban solution. Smaller versions of this block existed in many 'western' cities, but their concrete mix was usually of a higher grade. This catastrophe in mass housing had shed great lumps of its skin and in many places the iron skeleton was showing. To protect pedestrians from the rain of debris, a skirt of netting swirled about its first storey, like tulle on a ballet dress. Although the building was boarded up it still had its denizens whose lights could be seen flickering on the higher floors at night.

The second reason for the tram ride was the Trummerberge – two hills in the Volkspark known as Mont Klamott. When Berlin was rebuilt after World War Two the rubble was heaped into 'mountains' in parks and outlying areas and then grassed over. This was one of them. Something I thought said much about the pragmatism of the German soul.

From there the route went down the Unter den Linden, through the Brandenburg Gate, past the Reichstag and the concrete oyster known as the Haus der Kulturen der Welt to the main station, and back to our apartment at the top of what Christopher Isherwood called the boring section of the Ku'damm.

Summer lasted until the end of September and then suddenly it was autumn. Never before had I seen such a dramatic change of season: the trees went russet, brown, yellow and then shed all these crisp, flaky colours onto the pavements, into the hedges and the gardens. For week after week the very fabric of the sky seemed to be peeling away and falling. I discovered the pleasure of walking through leaf pile. I was entranced. I stood at the kitchen window and looked up into the canopy of a plane tree two storeys higher and watched it fragment at first slowly, day by day, then faster as Siberian winds shook loose the more tenacious leaves. Within an hour the upper floors of an apartment block across the back gardens that had been invisible for six months were back in sight. In the courtyards banks of leaves drifted against the fences and the bicycle racks; the streets were truly golden. There was a new sound, too: the scratch of leaves against the window panes; the scrape of someone sweeping. And then the streetsweepers arrived on their motorised vacuum cleaners to hoover away an autumn that was threatening to bury us.

For all the charm of this season, it also meant that the tree outside the study window became increasingly skeletal again. A reminder of bleak days.

Berlin in autumn proved as ambiguous as it had been in summer. I still felt trapped by the city but I was also continually seduced by the season. The walks I'd never taken in the Tiergarten I now took two or three times a week to admire the ochre of the turning trees. I went more often to Wannsee and to the island of Pfaueninsel and the deserted beach at Nikolassee. Everywhere were summer's remains: a glass forgotten on a windowsill, a board with mid-September water temperatures chalked up, stacks of deckchairs awaiting winter storage, pedalos hauled into a wire enclosure.

In November came savage periods of cold. It was back to coats, scarves and gloves every time we went out, and the central heating was now on constantly. Then, unexpectedly, the city came to our rescue. We discovered more cinemas showing movies in English, music

cafés in Kreuzberg, and every Tuesday and Friday a.
the Turkish street market that set up along the Landwei.
it slid through Kreuzberg to buy cheeses, fish, halva, olives, a.
Berlin seemed to have taken pity on us. For two months the ci,
us gently, offering unexpected concerts and an extraordinary art v
hibition – a retrospective of the work of Germaine Richier. Her metal
sculptures were of half-human, half-insect figures caught within the
webs they created.

'Do you not think these are about Berliners and the nature of our
city?' asked Thomas with a straight face. 'We are so expert at trap-
ping ourselves.'

I stared at Richier's work: the straining spider woman with thread
stuck to her fingers and her toes; the praying mantis begging for
release. They weren't going anywhere and were being consumed with
longing. They were so thin, their skins corroded and lumpy, sometimes literally eaten away. It came as a surprise to learn that Richier
had made most of them in Paris in the forties. I couldn't imagine
these creatures existing anywhere other than Berlin.

'I must tell my nephews and nieces to see this exhibition,' said
Thomas when we sat in a café afterwards drinking coffee. 'It is a new
idea about the Internet for them.'

If Richier was about Berlin – and about how I felt in Berlin – then so
was the work of the United States sculptor Kienholz. The city hosted
a retrospective of his installations – many made in Berlin, which he'd
adopted as a second home. Often in his installations I saw a light
and sensed a raw sadness that I knew from my wanderings about
Berlin's streets. One piece in particular – called Sollie 17 and mod-
elled after an Idaho residential hotel – was the epitome of my understanding of Berlin. You walked down the hotel corridor to a door
slightly ajar, and, with all the thrill and guilt of a voyeur, glanced
in on an old man wearing only a pair of ill-fitting Y-front underpants.
The man was in three positions: he lay on a bed reading a trashy
novel, he sat dejectedly on the edge of the bed, and stared out the
window on a grey industrial scene. The light bulbs were unshaded
but the light was dim. The bed, a trolley cluttered with cooking uten-
sils, a dressing table, and the three figures suggested a claustrophobia that was almost unbearable. The sort of claustrophobia I'd only

...n in Berlin. I was drawn to this scene even as I wanted to
...nastily away. The old man in Sollie 17 was a warning. You see
...ne, he said, you see yourself. The question though was how to avoid
that Idaho/Berlin residential hotel? Neither the old man nor Kienholz had any ready answers. Although Thomas suggested that having a good retirement plan was obviously essential.

During these final weeks Jill and I took to eating Sunday lunch at
the Deutsche Historischer Museum on the Unter den Linden. I suppose it was something about the marble floors and columns, the potted tree ferns, the waiters in their long white aprons, and the windows that looked onto an array of ancient cannons in the courtyard
that attracted me. Let alone the Russian missile in the entrance hall,
reminding us of what, not long ago, was aimed at the western part
of the city. Afterwards, we would sally on to the Unter den Linden
and parade up and down with the Berliners, as they'd done in the
first decades of the century. Who could ever believe what that av-
enue had seen: from Hitler's goose-stepping troops to those of the
GDR? Vanished now, although for me the ghosts lingered.

I had hoped that leaving Berlin would be leisurely and give us a
chance to remember our year. It had been an uncomfortable, restless time when I was constantly aware of not being at home. I was
no refugee, but I was alienated by the city. The huge urban conur-
bation unrelieved by any natural characteristics – except for the
forests and the lake of Wannsee which merely served to emphasise a
feeling of claustrophobia – had hemmed me in. Something had happened during the year, I wasn't quite sure what, but in a sense there
would be no going back to the life I'd known. Although I wasn't
prepared to admit this either then or in the months to come.

Certainly the final hours in Berlin didn't allow for much intro-
spection. Instead they spun into a gasping rush of panic. The bank
account had to be closed. The final telephone bill paid at the post
office. A present delivered to the urbane Thomas. 'I will see you in
Cape Town,' he said. The pot plants had to be taken downstairs to
Mohammed, who couldn't go home to Algeria because he was on a
hit-list there. The jars of small change we'd accumulated over the
year had to be divided among his children. A stack of *New Yorker*

magazines had to go upstairs to Aris, who was only returning to Stockholm in the new year. A half-full bottle of olive oil, unused packets of pasta, unfinished bottles of jam and honey were dispensed up and downstairs. I still had papers to sort through but never got round to them and ended up dumping the lot. Unaccountably, through the morning we generated large bags of rubbish which had to be emptied into the bins in the courtyard: glass, brown and clear; glass, green; paper; tins; the rest. All this took valuable time that could have been spent mulling over a year in Berlin. But no, I was hurtling from apartment to courtyard in our mania to leave everything spotless. The temperature was minus five degrees centigrade, yet I was sweating like a bricklayer.

Despite a shower I was still overheating when the taxi arrived to take us to the airport. In fact I was having some difficulty keeping a grip on events, especially as fluster was not my natural state. When the taxi pulled off I found I'd left my laptop and my shoulder bag with our passports and air-tickets on the study desk. Patiently the taxi-driver reversed and even switched off the meter while I raced upstairs.

At Tegel there was one last obstruction to overcome. The retractable handle of my recently purchased bag on wheels wouldn't retract. I pushed at it, hit it, asked the baggage handler to use violence on it, but the handle was intractable. Sweat was now pouring from me. I felt rivers coursing from my armpits and soaking my T-shirt. I surrendered. I pictured the handle jamming into the side of a conveyor belt and ripping open the fabric of the bag. But what could I do? Behind me people in the queue were shuffling their feet, the check-in clerk was about to ask if I could continue the fight some place else. I let go of the handle and the bag was consigned to the Fates.

For the next fifteen minutes Jill and I sat quietly trying to regain a sense of calm. I gazed at Tegel's inner circle, clogged with taxis. A digital noticeboard gave the time and showed a temperature of minus six degrees C. This was not the way I'd wanted to leave Berlin. A few moments solemn thought for the city that had affected our lives in ways we were yet to discover was what I'd wanted. Not this frazzled perspiring state of agitation. Yet could it have been any other way?

3: *The Stuff Of Paranoia*

On the morning we arrived home Cape Town was clearing after a night of rain. The mountains still had rags of cloud draped along them but the sky was intensely blue, newly washed. I stood in the summer sunshine of the airport car park wearing my long black winter coat, sweating, but no longer flustered. The puddles of rainwater hadn't evaporated yet. About me were the happy sounds of family reunions.

Our friends hustled us towards their car. We put our bags in the boot and flopped onto the back seat. The central locking system closed with a whine.

'Welcome home,' said our friends in unison, turning round. It felt rather like being welcomed to a foreign country by couriers who would wish us a nice day at the end of a short cautionary list of do's and don'ts. We gazed back at them expectantly.

'Just a few tips,' they said, 'because things have changed a little. Basically, don't drive with the doors unlocked. Keep the windows wound up when you stop at traffic lights. Be alert to what's happening around you. Don't stop too close to the car in front so you can drive round it should you need to. We've had a few hijackings recently. Nothing like Johannesburg but you don't want to take chances. Also there've been a series of Natural Born Killer-type killings. Awful stuff. Bodies dumped in the bush, that kind of thing.' They paused. 'It's so nice to have you back. Where would you like to breakfast?'

We drove down the peninsula to the Penguin Point Café at Boulders Beach and took a table on the deck with a view of the dazzling sea and the sweep of the False Bay mountains. The other tables were soon occupied by German and French and English tourists. From the hedges around the car park penguins emerged and waddled down to the rocks. Traders from Zimbabwe, Congo, Nigeria, Malawi set up stalls of curios, the seemingly endless trinkets that have become the stock of these markets: soapstone figures, leatherwork, masks, walking-sticks, beads, wooden spoons. The first coach load of Japanese sightseers arrived, led by a woman holding up a small flag on a stick. They disappeared between the hedges heading for the beach and the penguin colony.

Everything was as it had been.

After breakfast our friends drove us home. The moment we entered Muizenberg I could see that everything was not as it had been. For some years Muizenberg had been in decline, restaurants closed and rowdy bars opened, many of our neighbours fled to the suburbs as the slum landlords bought up property and the 'ghetto's' former quaintness took on the rough edge of what the sociologists call 'a transition phase'. I was surprised at just how much transition there'd been during our year away.

Our street was littered with broken bottles, half bricks, discarded shoes, the wrecks of cars. Men loitered in groups on the corners, music blared from windows. Babies crawled in the gutters, children played cricket in the middle of the road using tins as stumps. Women in curlers stood at their gates smoking. I groaned. I wasn't ready for this. I also knew I wouldn't ever be ready for this.

We reached our house.

For sixteen years, all through my thirties and into my forties, Muizenberg had meant a great deal to me. I had been infatuated with the place, intrigued by its characters, so at home that I thought I would only leave in a coffin. I had lived nowhere else longer than I'd lived in Muizenberg.

I went there because the houses were cheap and charming and the resort somewhat sleazy, but in a derelict rather than a nasty way. Even in those days it was a hard-drinking neighbourhood: on the stoeps imbibing cheap wine from tea cups sat a variety of Neanderthal types – men in vests and shorts, women in curlers and petticoats – who I later discovered existed from one disability pension payout to the next. Or more specifically from one bottle of brandy to the next. But to me they added a fascinating dimension. Far from being put off, I was enticed.

We moved into a house where we found unspeakable filth everywhere and dead rats decaying beneath the floor boards. Undaunted, a lengthy process of renovation began.

Over the years converting the house, giving it a new dignity and making it our home became a dream on which we spent all our spare cash, not to mention a considerable amount of energy.

And as a slow tarting-up started throughout the area we were content.

Muizenberg had a long history – in colonial terms – going back some two hundred and fifty years. Before that the caves and rock overhangs on the mountainside had offered shelter to Khoi and Bushman groups, just as the sea must have yielded a rich harvest of molluscs and lobsters. But the recorded history began in the 1740s when the Dutch East India Company stationed a watchman there to warn the garrison in Cape Town should any troublesome British ships slip in and try to attack the settlement by dispatching troops overland. Late in the eighteenth century the Company's fear came true. In 1795 three British ships entered the bay and the Dutch and Khoi troops sent to deter them proved no match. They offered some desultory musket fire but fled at the first broadside from the British man-o'-war. Some went over the mountain, no mean feat as it was a lung-wrenching climb. Some headed back towards Cape Town. Today a suburb called Retreat marks where they were captured. The incident became known as the Battle of Muizenberg – although battle is perhaps a rather grandiose term for a rout. Nevertheless an important rout as it signals the transition of the Cape from a Dutch to a British possession.

From then until early in the twentieth century, Muizenberg was little more than a homestead with vegetable gardens and a dairy herd. Urbanisation only started with the influx of Lithuanian Jews in the first two decades of that century. To them the resort owed its character: not only its architecture but the eccentric layout of narrow streets. In the forties and fifties they gave it, too, a reputation as Cape Town's Riviera.

The descendants of that original community virtually abandoned Muizenberg in the sixties in favour of the warmer, less windy northern parts of the peninsula. But some kept beach homes there and, until recently, over the summer holidays Muizenberg would regain something of its former character with families parading through the streets or heading off to the synagogue on Friday evenings.

At one time I believed those founders cast on the area a sense of community. There was a spirit of goodwill in the neighbourhood and a tolerance of some eccentric characters: a woman who always carried chickens in her coat pocket; a bearded prophet who wandered around with a placard proclaiming the end of the world; Eddie the Mercenary with his tales of mayhem, murder and pillage in the Congo; Hotnot the bergie; or Mr Adams of Mons Tuck Shop – although he was murdered some years ago for the money in his till.

These characters were, for me, the essence of Muizenberg. They were walking stories and they could draw you into their narrative in abrupt and unexpected ways. Quite simply popping out to the corner store could entail extraordinary revelations should one of these people be about.

I first encountered Eddie the Mercenary in Mons Tuck Shop. It was late on a Friday night. I'd gone in to buy milk. As I entered he rushed towards me, extending his hand: 'Hi,' he said, 'I'm Eddie the Mercenary.' Such an introduction clearly didn't strike him as out of the ordinary. And by then I'd lived in Muizenberg long enough not to bat an eye. We shook hands. 'I served in the Congo with Mad Mike Hoare,' Eddie the Mercenary continued, 'you know the famous Mike Hoare. We were given a thousand rand by the South African government to fight there. You see this.' He showed me something that looked like a piece of steel piping. It was about ten centimetres long. At the flick of a switch it extended into a lethal weapon. 'With this I can kill somebody,' he said swishing it about. Perhaps he could. Perhaps he had. Mr Adams smiled owlishly at us from behind his counter. On Friday nights Mr Adams always wore a medal that the then Soviet President Mikhail Gorbachev had sent him in recognition of his kindness to Russian soldiers in Europe at the end of World War Two. I paid for the milk and wished them both goodnight. 'See you, china,' said Eddie the Mercenary, lunging and feinting with his lethal weapon. This sort of moment was pure Muizenberg.

As was this: I was returning from the library one Saturday morning when a well-spoken man accosted me.

'Good, Sire,' he said – and I'm not kidding – 'pray can you give me the sum of R1000?'

I looked startled.

'Then, pray, good sir, money for bread?'

I declared my penury.

'But, sire,' he continued unabashed, 'for two weeks now my nose has not stopped bleeding. Why do you think I ail?'

What could I say?

Or: I am confronted by a hirsute sort who declares that he will read me the sonnet he has just composed – in rhyming couplets – if I will part with the price of a bottle of beer.

This hirsute sort was white and a loner, a tramp of long standing in the area. He kept to himself whereas most of the other down-and-outs eventually ended up in the company of a bunch of bergies. They were an ugly, nihilistic group who spent every cent they begged on cheap sweet wine. For some reason they were particularly attracted to Muizenberg, possibly because the bush on the lower slopes of the mountain formed a thick canopy, a shelter, which kept out all but the worst of the winter storms. But possibly also because Muizenberg had two bottle stores.

Once while wandering the slopes in search of some fortifications built by the Dutch in the eighteenth century, I strayed into what could best be described as a bergie house. In one room – for a room it was albeit with a leafy roof and walls of bushes – were some armchairs much the worse for wear but still serviceable. In another was a bed, and a third served as a kitchen. No one was at home but I felt decidedly like a trespasser tip-toeing through these neatly swept rooms.

A resident of the mountain with whom I used to have occasional conversations was a piratical figure called Hotnot. To the politically correct Hotnot is a derogatory term but Hotnot insisted on being known by this name and I suspect that in some subtle way he was really making fun of me. Hotnot could be savagely frightening, especially when he was drunk on blue train, that lethal concoction of meths strained through white bread. But when he was only mildly intoxicated he was very funny.

Once, while negotiating for a fish called a hottentot at Kalk Bay harbour, who should leer over the table but Hotnot himself. 'You mustn't call them hottentot,' he informed me, 'this is the new South Africa, you must call them Cape silver bream. And us Cape silver bream people don't like being called by what you just called that fish.' He grinned toothlessly at me from his small wrinkled face and then was off in that disjointed walk of his, cackling with amusement.

This was the Muizenberg I had valued. A home to people like Hotnot but also to a host of artists, musicians, writers, computer programmers, potters, and a number of old age pensioners. Mostly, as I've said, gone, as we should have gone years ago. But we kept holding out, hoping Muizenberg would pass quickly through the 'transition phase' and return to being a little Soho. From what I'd seen as we returned home, our new neighbours didn't share this vision.

Home was different too. It smelt the same: an old mustiness mixed with sea damp. It looked the same: the clutter of books and pictures and furniture. But I felt as much an interloper walking in as I'd felt on first entering the Berlin apartment. I stood in the hall, confused. This wasn't my home anymore. I didn't belong. I was merely a temporary sojourner, a man passing through. This was a deeply unsettling feeling.

Then Jill exclaimed, 'Our house has shrunk. It's so small. I never realised our house was so small.' She reached out her hands to touch the passage walls. She laughed. That hollow non-laugh people make when they're disconcerted.

By many standards the house wasn't small. I had a study and an extra room. There was our bedroom, a walk-in dressing room, a guest bedroom. A sitting room, two bathrooms, kitchen, dining room. Nothing palatial but more than enough space for two people. Yet now as we began to explore our own home we bumped into furniture, unable to adjust to rooms that after the spacious volumes of the Storkwinkel apartment seemed crowded.

Distracted, not talking, we unpacked. Again I had the sensation of being displaced. Of being a refugee who had no control over his situation and lived within the whim of mysterious forces. There'd been a reason to feel like this in Berlin but this was supposed to be home.

Jill made coffee and we sat at the dining-room table. I opened the doors on to the courtyard where the lavender was in bloom and the bougainvillaea a bright crimson, and orange flowers on the Cape honeysuckle waited for the sunbirds. Above us rose Muizenberg mountain. All this was familiar. Had been familiar for fifteen years.

Jill sighed. 'I'm a stranger in my own house,' she said.

Unfortunately the feeling didn't go away.

And over the next few weeks we probably made it worse. To begin with there was the Burglary. Everything looked as we'd left it yet intermittently we realised odd items were missing: an iron, electric hairclippers, old watches, electric extension leads. Were the miscreants still sneaking into the house the moment we went out? (The robber-kids had never gone to trial, having escaped over the prison wall shortly after being arrested. At the back of my mind was the persistent thought: would they come back to reclaim what they'd tried to steal?) Such thoughts, of course, are the stuff of paranoia. And paranoia is as catching as the common cold. From neighbours we learnt that opportunistic break-ins occurred frequently. Daily by their counts. All you had to do was step out for the newspaper and by the time you returned your hi-fi would be gone. This implied scheming eyes everywhere. 'Oh yes,' said the neighbours, 'we're being watched.' Claustrophobia struck. I was reluctant to leave the house. I felt imprisoned.

4: 'In My Country There Are Many Troubles'

During the closing months of my stay in Berlin I'd been convinced that within six weeks of being back I would have picked up the old routines as if the year away had never happened. Whenever someone said, 'You'll find it difficult settling down again' I shook my head, amazed at the suggestion. But I wasn't settling down. I couldn't get back into the old routine.

My usual summer days went like this: early in the morning we would walk along the coastal way to the tidal pool at St James for a swim. Shortly after nine we'd return home. If the southeaster hadn't worked itself into a gale by the late afternoon we would swim again, this time off Muizenberg beach. Not a difficult routine to fall back into, one would think.

Except I was beset with worry: would the house be safe while we were out? Would someone notice our routine? Would our clothes be stolen from the beach during our swim? This was no way to live, I chided myself. You have to keep the paranoia levels under control.

You can't cower inside, you've got to face the world. I kept on repeating this like a mantra.

On two successive mornings we did the St James walk. But what had once been a careless, relaxed start to the day was now spoilt by a tick of anguish at the back of my mind. So we hurried there and we hurried back. Nor did I enjoy the walk. Graffiti defaced the coastal path, even the rocks were sprayed with the nonsensical patterns that had been used to vandalise so many cities throughout the world. Such viciousness irritated me. Worse, made me angry. Apart from this, the litter worked me up. I couldn't stand the sight of plastic bags in the rock pools, smashed bottles, chicken bones in the sand, and everywhere cigarette butts more numerous than shells. Even the bergies strung out along the way were getting to me. I grimaced at their foul language, I was more than annoyed by their begging. I cringed inwardly every time I heard the mucus rasp of someone about to hawk up.

On the third morning Jill said, 'You go. I can't deal with these issues first thing in the morning.'

I remembered a passage in Mario Vargas Llosa's *The Real Life of Alejandro Mayta* about the misery of the slums spreading throughout the city of Lima even into the exclusive residential suburbs. 'If you live in Lima, you can get used to misery and grime, you can go crazy, or you can blow your brains out,' he wrote. Same sentiments, different city. Neither of us was getting used to the misery and grime; we were both going crazy.

Before we blew our brains out the early morning walks to St James pool stopped. When we wanted a swim we drove down to the sedate cleaner beach at Fish Hoek. What I resented about this was being forced out of 'my' Muizenberg for the pleasures of a swim, and having to use a car.

Muizenberg had been one of the few places I'd lived where it was possible to get by without a car. There were shops, restaurants, and for many years a reliable train service through to town which made a car an optional extra. I always ran a car but occasionally it wouldn't be used for days on end. Now a car was vitally important. It was the main item on our shopping list. Fortunately our garage-man found a vehicle for us fairly quickly.

Initially the disturbing thing about our 'new' car was that the doors wouldn't lock. They wouldn't lock because the central locking system was broken. And the reason the central locking system had broken was because after twenty years car parts tend to break.

Uppermost in my thoughts while I considered buying this car was the warning: 'Don't drive with your car doors unlocked. Someone may put a gun in your ear.'

What should I do? Turn down the offer? I thought the car would be a fine acquisition. It had power-steering, an automatic transmission, it was huge. Cheap too. Our garage-man patted the roof. 'How about this?' he said triumphantly.

This was a 1978 Mercedes Benz-250. An unusual model. But with enough spread to the bonnet, and enough chrome trim to make driving seem a completely serene and grand activity.

'A genuine ninety thousand kilometres,' confirmed the garage-man.

I eyed him dubiously. 'Who'd it belong to? An old man who drove it up and down his drive-way?'

'More or less,' he replied. 'Truly.'

Even if the odometer should have read double that, it was a good deal. I also trusted the garage-man. He knew a sound car when he saw one.

'What about the door locks?' I asked.

'Tell you what,' he said, 'drive it around for a week or so then bring it in and I'll fix up any little problems.'

'We can't drive around without door locks.'

'Course you can,' he responded, slipping me the invoice. 'Be brave.' I wrote him a cheque for sixteen thousand rand to show I wasn't a coward.

'What about the door locks?' asked Jill when we were alone. 'What about the Natural Born Killers?'

I shrugged. 'Be brave,' I said.

For six weeks we were brave. Every time I stopped at a traffic light I would scan the rear-view and side mirrors for hijackers. At any moment I expected rough hands yanking open the doors and hauling me out. When I parked in the street or at a shopping mall or at the beach I expected to return to a vandalised car. Or no car at all.

Then again, I tried to rationalise, why would anyone steal a sluggish old Merc?

A common answer among many alternatives presented by the various people I asked was, simply to get home. Why put up with an erratic public transport system or the suicidal mania of the minibus taxi drivers, when you could steal a car and calmly drive home? Why indeed?

While the car freed us from Muizenberg, this freedom was actually a loss. Muizenberg had been my home. I had felt as comfortable in its streets as I had in my living room. This sense of territory was gone now. The new inhabitants had usurped the streets.

Most of the new inhabitants were refugees, young men who'd fled the warring, hopeless regions of Africa. They rented mattress space from the slumlords and crowded twenty into unfurnished houses with one toilet, one bath, one basin between them. They took possession of the streets because there wasn't enough room in the houses. They spat, pissed, defecated, had sex before my eyes.

Hard-faced lowlifes had also moved in from Cape Town's other slum quarters. Graffiti appeared overnight on the walls: 'blood in, blood out' read one, ominous but at the same time incomprehensible and stupid. I was told of a crack house in the next street, a shebeen on the corner. I was told I could buy any drug going in the now misnamed Church Street. I no longer wanted to walk through the streets of Muizenberg. Not because they were dangerous but because I couldn't stand the filth, the noise, the sights. The beach, too, became a no-go zone. Too much litter, too many uncouth drunken people, too many full-volume car radios playing funk. Not the sort of beach for a leisurely afternoon swim.

Muizenberg no longer had anything to offer me. Which was when I should have reconciled the unease that had started in Berlin with my loss of Muizenberg and understood the message. But I didn't want to. I wasn't going to give up on Muizenberg that easily. I might feel alienated. I might abhor the misery and grime, but before it drove me crazy I should at least know something about the lives that contributed to the misery and grime. Maybe empathy would help me adapt. I decided to find out about the refugees.

Down the street a hairdressing salon had opened recently. It was decked out in hairstyle fashion posters and the unsmiling glare of Tupac Shakur. Some product lines were haphazardly arranged on the shelves, and for some obscure reason two bales of hay served as window dressing. The salon was an instant success, it was also a social centre where impeccably dressed young men gathered in the afternoons to listen to music and talk. They played battered cassette tapes of much-loved singers in their home countries and they played them loudly. I couldn't understand how they managed to hear one another above the noise yet they always seemed to be engrossed in animated conversations. From the outside there was no visible grief in their lives.

One afternoon I went in and started talking with an Angolan who'd taken a job as a 'stylist' – his word – in the salon. He'd been in Muizenberg a few weeks and shared a room with three other men. His name was Robert Carlo. He was twenty years old. A small-boned, quiet man with a ready smile. During a break between clients, with reggae singer Lucky Dube at such volume on the boombox I could barely hear his soft-spoken story, Robert told me that he'd left Angola because it offered no future. We shared problems, I saw, although his were of a greater order. His English was halting but he knew enough to articulate his circumstances and, possibly because he had only a limited vocabulary, the details were all the more poignant.

'In my country there are many troubles,' he began. 'I know my country well, I know those people will not solve the problems. I can remember the bad times and I need a new life.'

For his first fifteen years Robert lived in Luanda. His father worked in the city as part of a Unita delegation negotiating with the MPLA government towards a peaceful settlement. Sometimes, if the talks broke down or the situation became tense, the Carlo family felt the repercussions. On one occasion, Robert came home from school to find their house gutted and his mother and sister wandering in shock among the smouldering ruins.

Shortly afterwards he was sent to relatives in a northern province where for the next four years he worked as a builder, learning the trade on the job. But this was not the life he wanted. He'd been trained as a hairdresser in Luanda and he missed city living. Then he heard about Cape Town: no wars, apartheid over, a modern thriving economy. Robert Carlo resolved to head south.

He returned to Luanda, acquired travel documents and said goodbye to his family. It took him a week, walking and hitching rides on trucks, to reach Namibia. It took him three days to travel through Namibia and another two before he arrived in Cape Town.

'I like this place,' he said to me finally, 'it is better.'

By now a group of seven or eight men had gathered around us. Some of them shook their heads at his last statement.

'He has only been here a few weeks,' said one of the men. 'Me, I have been here five years and now I am going to Holland. It is too dangerous for us here. If we walk alone in the townships they will kill us. The blacks don't like us.'

'Cape Town is not home for us,' added a dapper man in a double-breasted suit. He told me he was from the Congo but wouldn't give his name. 'The Xhosa don't like black foreigners,' he explained. 'They say, give me R5. And if you don't give it they will kill you. What is this? How can you kill someone for R5? We can't stay in Langa or Guguletu because they will kill us if they find us there. The people here they drink too much, they want to kill too quickly, they are lazy, they don't work. Things are going to be bad here, very bad. The whites don't care and the blacks are bad. When Mbeki is president then it will be even more difficult for us. So many of us are going to leave South Africa before the elections. When I see new people come here I tell them they are crazy. I say why have you come here? It is better to stay at home than come here.'

Robert Carlo listened to the discussion with a serious face. He sat with his hands knotted in his lap not looking at the speakers but staring across the room into the mirrors on the far wall that reflected the group. The Lucky Dube tape was long finished yet no one noticed. The talk shifted to the killing of a man called Djo Ongonga Okamba just days before he was due to fly home. Okamba, who'd lived in Muizenberg, had been shot the previous night in the Johannesburg suburb of Yeoville by a man known as 'Coloured'. The story was that 'Coloured' had already killed two other Congolese and an Ethiopian. While the men exclaimed and gave vent to their anger at these senseless killings, Robert reached over and tapped my knee. 'My friend,' he said, 'I think for me it will be alright here in Cape Town.'

What Robert Carlo left out of his story were the horrors of war. A war that had been waged in his country since the late sixties and had devastated the people, their economy and turned the landscape into a hazardous terrain of unexploded landmines. Vast areas of Cape Town may be too dangerous for him to visit but compared with Angola the risks were minimal. Besides, Muizenberg gave him a safe haven, just as once, many decades ago, it provided Lithuanian Jews with a place to settle.

But while I had every sympathy for the refugees, what I couldn't understand was why they turned their immediate surroundings into a slum. These well-dressed, well-groomed young men thought nothing about throwing litter out of the window into the street. Just as they thought nothing about pissing against our back wall. The houses they rented deteriorated daily simply because there were too many people sitting on the walls and leaning from the windows. They lived in appalling circumstances yet refused to improve their lot. Meanwhile they dragged down Muizenberg for all of us.

5: A Hell Of A View

For five months we tried to come to terms with Muizenberg but the feeling of being trapped and unsettled persisted. Jill was in despair and no matter how much we talked about the situation there seemed to be no way out. Eventually, on one desperate Sunday morning we took our troubles to a friend who also looked after our finances. Over breakfast at a Noordhoek restaurant he heard out our woes. His advice was to move. Something had come to an end, something new had to be started. For a finance man he had a mystic turn of mind. More importantly he was right. If we were to reclaim some peace we would have to leave Muizenberg. But how? We didn't have the capital. 'I'll arrange a loan,' he said. 'We'll take it from there.'

What he did I now see was push us in a direction we'd been fearful of going. As it was our initial steps into the unknown were tentative. I tried to hang on to Muizenberg even as Jill made appointments to look at houses. But gradually we entered the lengthy, tedious, disappointing process that is called 'house-hunting' – hunting because the prey is secretive and elusive.

The house we were hunting had to have a view of the bay, which cut down the options. Then, almost as a matter of course, we weren't interested in a new house because generally new houses were badly designed and unattractive. One, which should have had fine sea views, crouched behind a high wall. Only in the dining room, if you stood on a chair, could the sea be seen through the top right-hand corner of a window.

'What sort of house are you after?' the estate agents would ask in exasperation as we shook our heads yet again.

Actually our intentions were altogether more esoteric than the estate agents could ever have realised. We were looking for neither a house nor a home. We were searching for a new way of life. This became increasingly clear each weekend as we scanned through the property pages of the newspaper selecting adverts that read: 'Graceful Victorian lady needs tlc ...' or 'old whaling cottage with oodles of charm' or 'a delightful gem from yesteryear with Oregon pine floors' or 'sea views framed by a bay window of leaded cottage panes'.

These 'delightful opportunities' (as one agent put it) were 'realistically priced' (to use another's terminology) in the region of our budget yet they needed to be renovated. Even allowing for some haggling we might have come out with a little change in the case of the whaling cottage and the bay window, but the gem and the lady would have put us in hock. And without exception they were small houses, half of what we had with no chance of expanding.

'We'll have to stay in Muizenberg,' Jill said in frustration as we drove away from the cottage with leaded panes. 'But if that's the only alternative then we're going to radically change the house. Go up. Build an en suite bathroom so that we don't have to walk from one end of the house to the other in the middle of the night to use the loo. Build a garage so that we don't have to park our car half a kilometre away. If we've got to stay trapped we can at least be trapped in some kind of comfort.'

I wasn't convinced matters had – or would – come to this. In the years when we'd renovated the house we'd been so enthusiastic about reshaping rooms and creating our way of living that we'd talked of one day building our own house. Maybe this was the new way of life we were after? But we had to see a good many more houses before the obvious dawned.

Then, in the Saturday property section of the newspaper, I found plots of land for sale in a coastal suburb farther down the peninsula called Glencairn Heights. We decided to have a look.

It was a still, bright winter's day. The sea dazzled. The air had a brittle clarity. In the shadows were cold dewy patches. The mountains across the bay stood out in sharp relief. We drove round the headland into the narrow Glencairn valley. A small crescent of beach. A wetland with a river reaching back up the valley. The old Glencairn houses facing north on the farther side of the valley. The new Glencairn Heights opposite facing south.

We rode slowly past the vacant plots going higher and higher but began giving less attention to these than to the view. Not only the seascape but views back into the mountains at the head of the valley. Eventually I stopped the car. We got out, stunned. Silence. No disco music. Nobody hawking up. No bergie swearing. No one lying comatose on the pavement. No one begging. No broken bottles, used condoms, discarded plastic or tins. But breaking into the silence the calls of francolin and guineafowl. I noticed other mountain birds: bulbuls, robins, sunbirds, white eyes. Two francolins came out of the bush and crossed the road into a garden.

It was idyllic. Impossibly idyllic. So much light and air and space. There had to be a catch: why hadn't this suburb been bought up, built up? Why weren't people clamouring to live here?

We drove around marking the plots we thought had potential on a survey map supplied by an estate agent. There weren't many. Because the sea view was to the side some houses were built outwards on stilts in an effort to extend beyond their neighbour. As a result they completely blocked off this aspect for anyone who might try to build on the site alongside. Nevertheless there were two or three options.

And then we turned into a cul de sac. On the left-hand side the penultimate plot had a for sale notice. The map showed a strange five-sided erf with a narrow fifteen metre road frontage. Almost a panhandle. I stopped the car next to the for sale notice, facing down the hill. I could see the vlei, the beach, and farther along the peninsula, Boulders Beach and the rocks at Miller's Point. A little into the bay was Roman Rock lighthouse. Beyond that rose Cape Hangklip, where from the beginning of the eighteenth century until slavery was abolished in 1834 a community of runaways had lived, free of bondage but never able to return home. In the distance the sea seemed to rise into the sky.

I tried to break a path onto the plot but it was so densely overgrown with fynbos and aliens that only a powerfully wielded machete would have made any inroads. To the side of the plot was a brown face-brick house shaped in a U with the two arms extending towards the sea. At the end of the nearest arm was a bedroom, at the end of the other arm, a lounge. The connecting passage between the two arms was glass and slightly raised: from there the view was ideal. Nevertheless the house was intimidating, flat-roofed with a damp brick-paved courtyard between the arms. As it was empty we snooped around. From the lawn I was able to bundu-bash my way onto the panhandle plot. I discovered that after gently sloping down the handle the topography plunged quite steeply into the pan. I liked this instantly. Here we would be away from the street, entirely in our own world. I stood still. A striped field mouse rushed across a small patch of vacant sand. The air was filled with birdsong. I heard the crackle of the mouse in the bush. At that moment I was convinced this was where we would have to live.

I rejoined Jill on the lawn of the vacant house. While we stood there a man wearing running shoes, baggy green tracksuit pants and a grey crewneck jersey appeared round the side of the house. We greeted him.

'I hope you don't mind us standing on your land,' I said. 'We needed to get some idea of this plot.'

He shrugged.

'It's a hell of a view,' I said.

'That's why people live up here,' he replied.

Not friendly, not entirely brusque either, but a little defensive.

'You thinking of buying the plot?' he asked.

'We've only just seen it,' I explained.

'I wanted to buy it,' he said. 'But the guy wouldn't sell it to me. Then while I was building my house' – he indicated a house higher up the slope above the face-brick – 'he came to me and said he was going to sell it. I told him I didn't have any money to buy it.'

By his tone he sincerely resented this turn of events.

'Do you own this house?' I asked jerking a thumb at the U-shape. He nodded.

'Whoever builds here's going to block out your view,' I commented.

'No,' he said. 'There's building regulations which say no one can build higher than the floor level of the house behind them.'

I looked at the sandy ground of the vacant plot visible through the fynbos not a metre below our feet. According to those regulations, and considering that we stood on a level with his floors, one would have to build an underground bunker.

'You sure?' I queried.

'Completely. How else do people get to keep the sea view?'

He hadn't smiled once during the conversation. He stood glaring at us, his face deadpan, his voice now decidedly unfriendly.

'Well, thanks for letting us stand on your property,' I said.

A few days later, after we had been back to the plot at least four times, I telephoned the estate agent and said we were thinking of submitting an offer. But first I wanted to know about the building height restriction rulings? He explained that we could build a house up to the mean height of the erf behind us. He said he would fax the municipal building regulations. I then told him about the man in the green tracksuit pants.

'Don't worry about him,' he said. 'He doesn't know what he's talking about. He's your side neighbour. The house behind you is across the road, higher up the mountain.'

'Technically he's higher up the mountain, too,' I argued.

'That's not the way the town planners saw it,' the agent responded. 'In terms of their scheme he's to your side.'

The building regulations confirmed the agent's explanation, but I still wasn't happy. I approached the local building control officer. He confirmed the position. 'Ok,' said Jill, 'let's do it.'

6: One Thousand Square Metres

On a wet Friday morning in July I went to the estate agency and filed an offer to purchase.

The agent looked at me dubiously.

'The seller's a wealthy businessman,' he said, insinuating that he would reject out of hand an offer as trivial as mine.

'The market's stagnant,' I countered. The agent was doing mental arithmetic to calculate how much less commission he'd earn. 'Either the wealthy businessman wants to sell or he doesn't.'

The agent shrugged. 'Let's see what he says.'

I had no great confidence the offer would be accepted. I could hear the estate agent advising his client to hold out for the full amount because these were serious buyers, not bored speculators wanting to expand their property portfolio, but foolish people flying in the face of dire economic conditions. After all he hadn't had to sell us the plot or its potential. We walked in off the street and gave him business without his raising a finger. The proverbial money for jam.

Over the weekend Jill became ill with shingles. After suffering from back pain and feeling miserable all week, she spent the Saturday in bed. Late in the afternoon some small inflamed patches appeared on her thigh and waist. Two days earlier a doctor had warned that shingles was a possibility but without any obvious symptoms couldn't make a diagnosis. Jill phoned her, described the spots, and the doctor pronounced shingles without a doubt. But with a course of antibiotics the virus could be stopped within three days, she said. After three days the virus might have been killed but Jill literally writhed for a further week.

Yet those ten days also contain memories of peace and intimacy. One of the few things I could do for her was read aloud. For some reason my voice sent her to sleep within minutes. The book I read to her – a book I would probably never otherwise have read – was Wilkie Collins's opium novel, *The Moonstone*. It was a novel that, like all Victorian novels, demanded a lot of time.

Reading aloud was an unexpected pleasure. In the age of mass-produced entertainment an activity that was intimate, mutually rewarding and leisurely had been lost. Reading aloud had all the intensity of a love-triangle: book, reader, listener – each one intent on creating a fantasy world. So while Jill battled against a biting pain, the pedant, Gabriel Betteredge, drew us deeper and deeper into what was really little more than a soap opera. But we went willingly, relishing the sheer unhurried telling of the story. And no matter where I left off there was always an urgent question dangling over the narrative: What's going to happen now?

The Moonstone was my first reintroduction to 'genre' fiction since adolescence when cowboys, detectives, thrillers, and spy stories were the staple of my reading. Then the earnestness of a writing life set me on the straight and narrow of serious literature and, being a good disciple, I never wavered. But a smoked-up Wilkie Collins expanded my mind. For, apart from his sheer inventive pleasure in shaping the narrative and his use of literary devices that would look respectable in any self-consciously post-modern work, he showed that my snobbish disdain for the crime novel wasn't only misplaced, it was arrogant. The crime novel offered ways to describe a violent world that I'd ignored, it also imbued its setting – inevitably a city – with moods and secrets and ways of operating.

Over the following months I found my way to the LA of Raymond Chandler and James Ellroy, Elmore Leonard's Miami, James Lee Burke's New Orleans, and the dark New York streets of Lawrence Block and Ed McBain. For all of them the city was not a stage but a living organism where the life came as much from the citizens as from an innate presence. More than any other fiction the crime novel developed the city as a protagonist which fitted into my way of seeing Cape Town.

Some days later the estate agent telephoned to say the rich businessman had rejected our offer. Had it not been for Jill's condition we would undoubtedly have been shattered. Instead we simply said, too bad, and turned back to a more demanding issue. But as the shingles abated so our minds returned to Glencairn Heights. Should we pay the asking price and be damned? If we put in another lower offer would he simply throw it back? And how much lower could we go? Once I'd added up the conveyancing fees, the land surveyor's charge, and the site clearance cost we clearly had to come in lower simply to spend no more than our budget.

I went back to the estate agent and he amended the figures.

'He's a rich businessman,' he kept telling me. 'He's done these sort of negotiations all his life. Men like him just hang on until they get their price. He drives a hard bargain. Nerves of steel, you know.'

'Tell him we can't go any higher,' I said, trying not to sound as if I were pleading. 'That's it. Our final offer. If he's a serious seller that's the ceiling for us. This is already more than the average price in the area.'

The estate agent shrugged. 'I'll get back to you,' he said, shaking my hand. He stood up from his desk but didn't bother to see me out.

I went home to the ghetto not altogether optimistic. The contract gave the seller three days to decide. How were we going to live through three days, waiting? If he were playing cat and mouse he'd sit it out knowing that eventually, unable to stand the tension, we'd capitulate. He was faced with a minor investment issue, we seemed to be confronting our very lives. There was great inequality here. Too much was stacked in his favour. I hadn't been home half an hour when the phone rang.

'It's a done deal,' the estate agent said.

Calmly, trying to keep my voice even, I expressed my thanks.

'He took a lot of convincing,' the agent continued, determined to let me know what a job he'd done on our behalf. 'At first he wasn't interested. But I said what did it matter to him? In the end I had to take a lower commission to get him to agree.'

I made no comment.

'A pleasure doing business with you,' he said, ringing off.

The idea of owning one thousand square metres on the side of a mountain with a view of the sea took time to acquire meaning. In very real terms possessing land which we were going to develop meant entering a new relationship with the city. Our Muizenberg house had been built in the twenties. By owning and living in it I felt we were continuing the ways of an established part of the city. By building a new house we were adding to the city, saying this is our contribution.

First we had to set about claiming the land. Or rather I contracted others to go through the processes of 'claiming' the land as the plot was overgrown with alien vegetation. For a day a team of men wielded chain saws and axes and by evening I realised that what we'd bought had a very steep slope in the middle. Virtually a one in three drop. Also some extremely large rocks lay scattered around. Nothing short of a bulldozer would shift them, the clearance contractor speculated, gently kicking at one as if to emphasise its immovability. Then he kindly reassured me that building would cost a fortune on a plot this steep. But he supposed the view might be worth the price.

Next I hired a land surveyor to establish the boundary pegs and determine the contours. 'You're going to have problems with your neighbour,' he informed me. He meant the man in the green track suit pants, who had also bothered the clearance contractor for information about our plans. 'He's jumping around wanting to know what's going to happen. He's worried you're going to take away his view.'

I shrugged. 'The position of his house doesn't give us much leeway,' I said.

'Check out the regulations carefully,' the surveyor cautioned as he showed me the positions of the metal pegs. It was only then I saw that the piece of lawn I'd stood on when first viewing the plot hadn't belonged to the man in the green track suit pants. It was mine. I wondered if I should send him an invoice for rent.

The next part of the colonising process involved another friend, who, fortuitously, happened to be an architect. An architect who designed houses we both admired. He strode around the plot asking questions like: Did I want a view of the sea from the study window? No. Were the kitchen and dining room to be open plan? Yes. Would we mind the rafters showing? No. Did we want a sea view from the bedroom? Most certainly. Would we consider pursuing the briefing over coffee and chocolate croissants at the Olympia Café? Not at all.

In the café we added our dream house to the cacophony of conversations. The architect listened with a barely noticeable ironic detachment to descriptions of walk-in dressing rooms, flowing lounges, compact hi-tech kitchens, pantries, guest bedrooms, extra bathrooms, entrance halls, decks, French doors, and shutters. He waited until we were well down our cappuccinos before saying, 'I think you should allow yourselves a generous budget.' He named a figure which drained the blood from my face. 'Even then it's going to be tight,' he added. 'Not much elbow room.'

'We haven't got that,' I said.

'What do you mean tight?' said Jill.

'Don't worry,' he tried to reassure me, 'you'll get it in the end.'

7: An Aside 1

Towards the beginning of spring with the trees greening and the sun suddenly warmer, Thomas, our Berlin German teacher, came out for a short visit. We did all the tourist things with him: went up Table Mountain, drove down to Cape Point, wandered around the Waterfront, took the boat to Robben Island, stood on the scar of District Six, sat in coffee shops on St George's Mall. I gave him my Grim Guide to Cape Town as well which included Thornton Street in Athlone where police had used a 'Trojan Horse' to fire on civilians, and Klipfontein Road, which had been the site of running battles between township fighters and the security police, and the Heidelberg Tavern that had been shot up by PAC gunmen, killing four and severely wounding three others just four months before the general election in 1994. After a day of this Thomas was looking haggard.

'No,' he said, 'no more. I have my Berlin, you have your Cape Town. These are both cities full of pain but I think you must live with yours and I must live with mine. So tomorrow I wish to taste some wine.'

From a well-thumbed copy of John Platter's wine-guide – which he had bought in advance of his trip – he selected Middelvlei and Thelema as two estates he had to visit. The next day, in the car heading towards Stellenbosch, Thomas enthused about the dry finish of the Middelvlei pinotage and its raspberry aromas and mulberry undertones and the elegance of oak spices complementing the complexity with which the wine wandered around the palate – or some such wine talk. In Berlin I had learnt to make allowances for his poetic flights of fantasy.

'How do you know all this?' I asked.

'I have an interest,' he replied.

At Middelvlei we sat on the stoep sipping pinotage and watching the geese. Afterwards we wound up Hellshoogte to Thelema and a taste of wines that brought the word paradise to Thomas's lips. Across the road at Delaire we bought a picnic basket for lunch.

It was cool under the trees and the view down the valley had Thomas in raptures.

'You really have it tough,' he said with a slight edge of envy in his voice.

A few days later I took him out to Montagu as I had been commissioned to write a profile of the town for a travel magazine.

Where the road slid gradually towards the Breede River we stopped and I set up the gas plate and filled the Bialetti with dark French roast and lit the gas and stood in the solid quiet while the coffee percolated. Beyond were the Langeberg – light glistening like diamond brooches on the mountains where the sun caught wet rocks.

'This is most impressive,' said Thomas.

We continued in silence through Bonnievale towards the mountains and Cogman's Kloof – the narrow poort between the mountains that formed a natural entrance to the Little Karoo. At the start of the poort a small tunnel had been blasted through the rock and above this sat an English fort built by the jittery soldiers who survived the wholesale slaughter of Magersfontein in December 1899. Eight hundred killed by the Boers in a single morning.

'This is because the Boers had the famous German Mauser rifle,' commented Thomas laconically.

In Montagu we checked into the hotel and while Thomas rested I went on to the streets in search of interesting material.

At a service station and car dealership I spoke to a man who smoked long ultra light cigarettes. He wore a chunky ring and a gold chain round his neck. He told me that once Montagu was in your blood you would always have to return no matter how far in the world you travelled. He, himself, had spent many years in Cape Town trying to purge the town from his blood. Then, lying on his death bed after three heart attacks, he said to the Lord: 'Lord, I've had a good life, but if you give me a second chance I'll devote myself to those who need my help.' The Lord instructed him to return to Montagu and do good work in the townships. 'Montagu has a restfulness. This gets into you. I'll be buried here,' he said.

He lit another of the long ultra lights. He said he wanted to be buried next to his grandfather in the local cemetery. His grandfather was a legend in the district. During the Boer War his grandfather wore a dress and rode around the veld sniping at the English.

'He killed lots of men. He killed lots of men both during the war and afterwards,' said his grandson, proudly blowing ultra light smoke across the table towards me, the way smoke would clear from a Boer Mauser. Which might have impressed Thomas.

The car dealer's grandfather had been the district Field Cornet, the upholder of law and order. One rainy day while the Field Cornet was on the track of some robbers who'd filled their pockets at the bank, God revealed to him the awesome nature of divine justice. Now, according to the grandson, the Field Cornet could follow spoor better than any Bushman but he was having a hard time of it that rainy day because when it rains in the Karoo, really rains, then sloots that have been dry for years become raging torrents and the desert turns to water.

Somewhat daunted by rivers forming out of nowhere and confident that no one could find them in such miserable conditions, the robbers took shelter under an overhang. No sooner were they out of the rain than a mudslide cascaded down the koppie and completely buried them. All the Field Cornet found when he arrived was an arm sticking out of the mud.

'Next time you come to Montagu,' promised the Field Cornet's grandson, 'we'll go out there. You can still see the hand sticking out. It's a bit black and leathery now though.'

Someone – or rather something – else that found its way back to Montagu and now languished in an outhouse of the museum was the skull of a renegade called Koos Sas. It sat in a glass case on a velvet cloth and used to be an exhibit in the museum proper until some German tourists complained at this insensitivity and the skull was moved to the outside room. Leaning against the wall next to the skull was a photograph of Constable Jurie Dreyer who supposedly shot Koos Sas when he resisted arrest.

I thought the story of Koos Sas poignant, a quintessential late frontier story. Koos Sas was a Bushman. According to what little was known of his life he was a malcontent, in and out of jail, unable and maybe unwilling to find a place in a world of fences and laws. Sometimes he lived wild, sometimes he tried to live in a dorp but inevitably this led to trouble. After some months in the desert he found work at a trading store outside Montagu. For a few days all went well until some bottles of sweet wine disappeared. The trader, one Boetatjie Botha, accused Koos Sas of theft. Enraged, Sas beat the trader to the ground with a stump of wood and then cut his throat. Sas was arrested but escaped.

Five years later, early in 1922, seven hundred kilometres away near Springbok, Constable Dreyer, following the spoor of stock thieves, happened upon Sas's isolated hut. Recognising the fugitive from wanted posters, Dreyer returned the next day with a commando. Among the commando were the local dominee and his son who'd brought along a camera. Sas was cornered at his hut but, ever undaunted, screamed at the mounted police: 'You'll still have to eat a lot of bread before you catch me.' In the firefight that followed, Sas was shot dead. The constables posed with his body, while the dominee's son took photographs. They then buried Sas in a shallow grave and the commando returned to Springbok.

And that was where the story of Koos Sas would have ended, except that the dominee was fascinated by the dead outcast. As the months went by his obsession took on an urgent need to possess the bones of Koos Sas. Besides, as he intended applying to a North American university to study medicine, he believed the skeleton might provide clues to the Bushman's aberrant behaviour. So the dominee had the decomposing body disinterred and brought back to town and 'cooked in a large black soap-pot so that only clean bones remained,' as a local farmer recorded the incident.

The following year the dominee and his family sailed to North America – taking the bones of Koos Sas with them in a suitcase – where the dominee was to study medicine at the University of Louisville, Kentucky. After graduating in 1928, he went to Leiden, Holland, where he took the physician's examination before returning to South Africa in 1929. At some stage, either in the United States or in Holland, Koos Sas's skeleton, sans skull, may have been donated or abandoned in one of the institutions where the dominee studied.

Or the skeleton may have came back with the family and spent the next two decades in a box beneath the stairs of their house in a suburb of Cape Town. The dominee turned doctor practised medicine for many years before becoming a Member of Parliament. After his death in 1951 the Sas skull was donated by the dominee's family to the University of Stellenbosch. In the seventies the university in turn donated it to Montagu.

At first the skull of Koos Sas was kept on display in the local library, then moved to the museum when that was established in 1975. It joined the museum's other artefacts – mostly crockery, furniture, clothes, photographs, letters, watercolours, toys, doctors' implements, lamps, ornaments, farming tools, the bric-a-brac of white rural lives – until twenty years later the indignation of the German tourists had it relegated to the back room.

'I would agree with those compatriots of mine,' Thomas said quietly when I recounted the story of Koos Sas at supper that evening. 'We have a history of these sorts of things too.'

We were eating at a restaurant called Preston's because they served good food and wine, and had a black cat slipping between the tables.

We were there primarily because of the black cat.

Outside, and across the road, was a triangular road sign with a black cat on it. No where else in the country – or anywhere else – had I ever seen a road sign like this. Postcards of the road sign could be bought in the local cafés and tourist shops.

I was told by a teenager in the house next to the road sign that his mother had got the municipality to erect the sign after one of their cats was run over and killed. I thought this a fine thing for his mother to have done, and as his mother ran Preston's, this seemed to be a good reason to eat there.

Apart from the food and wine, our dinner was made memorable that evening by a couple's conversation at the next table.

She was wearing a blouse and a skirt and canvas shoes. He had on beige chinos and an open-necked shirt and a wind-breaker. They were late-thirtyish with west London accents and so probably tourists.

She said, 'I don't know why we have pubic hair anymore. You'd have thought after all these years we'd have got rid of unnecessary hair.'

'I suppose it was for protection once,' he replied between mouthfuls of roast lamb.

'But that was millions of years ago,' she said somewhat exasperated. 'We've been wearing clothes for ages.'

He swallowed some red wine and said, 'I must admit I've never seen the point either except perhaps as an area marker.'

She laughed. 'You mean that's why it's triangular, like a road sign.'

Thomas nudged me and said, 'Maybe we should tell Lilo Wanders about these two.'

For me Lilo Wanders had been a television highlight as the nights grew longer and darker towards the end of our stay in Berlin. She presented a satirical sex programme called Wa(h)re Liebe – true love, although the name was also a pun on the commercial opportunities (leather gear, vibrators, whatever) of sex. The quest Lilo Wanders had set herself was to reveal something of the sex lives of ordinary people. What amazed me was that so many ordinary people were prepared to welcome her – and her camera crew – into their bedrooms. Let alone go to the studio after they'd been filmed enjoying group gropes or whippings, to calmly discuss the ins and outs of their activities. What, I wondered, if you happened to switch on, only to see your daughter/son strapped to a bed while someone in black leather dripped hot wax onto places where it would surely hurt? Or, if you happened to switch on, only to see your mother/father strapped to a bed while someone in black leather ...?

I say Wa(h)re Liebe was satirical but Lilo Wanders's guests took their activities very seriously. None of them ever considered that the blonde with her piled-up hair, red lipstick, little-girl flouncy dresses and her long legs demurely crossed was taking the piss. None of them ever considered that they were talking to a happily married man with three kids whose male lover shared the family home. They would sit before her – plump and middle-aged or thin and twenty – clutching their bowl of fruit and explain in detail just where to put the banana for maximum satisfaction. With a slightly dreamy, isn't-love-beautiful expression, Lilo would smile. Her smile was nothing more than a lop-sided stretching of her lips, but it contained such bemusement at the foibles of men and women that I would ache with laughter.

Once, at an earnest Berlin dinner party, I was asked what I thought most succinctly summed up post-modern German culture. Without hesitation I answered, Lilo Wanders. My host almost choked. Thomas hid his smile behind a serviette. He then explained that this reaction said more about me and my country than about German intellectual acuity. 'Herr Nicol has lived in a repressed society all his life,' he told the dinner table. 'He suffers from years of censorship. It is to be expected that as soon as he sees a sex programme he will be attracted. Is this not so?' Thomas grinned at me. My host relaxed back in his chair, relieved. 'Of course,' I concurred, picking a kiwi fruit from a bowl and peeling it. Now what was it the woman said she did with a kiwi fruit ...?

Late the next morning we headed out of Montagu. The light was brittle, the heat building up and the mountain ranges shimmered along the distance. Thomas sighed that it was like driving into Jimi Hendrix's Purple Haze.

8: Perfect Timing

Once Thomas had returned to Berlin and life was back to its former anxieties, I began to wonder if buying the plot hadn't been a serious financial mistake. By the time lawyers and surveyors and clearance contractors and loan fees were paid we were seriously in debt. As a paramount condition of my writing life entailed living cheaply and having no debts, I was troubled.

And that was not the end of it. Suddenly the Asian stock markets crashed, sending devastating repercussions throughout the markets of the developing world, and local interest rates rose. Within weeks of taking out the loan at seventeen percent it had climbed to a gasping twenty-five percent. At that rate we could not meet the monthly commitments. In some consternation, a euphemism for 'in a blind panic', I met our financial friend.

'You'll live through this,' he said. 'In a few years you'll look back and these days of desperate unhappiness will simply be a good story. You'll be able to exaggerate it out of all proportion. Insinuate that you were close to a nervous breakdown. Tearing your hair out. Hollow-eyed from sleeplessness. At your wits' end. Absolutely frantic with worry. Isn't that how you writers depict life?' I could think of no suitable riposte.

Some days later the architect invited Jill and me to his office to view the sketch plans. With our hopes of ever paying off the plot dashed, our chances of affording a house weren't below the horizon, they were at the bottom of the sea. We felt wretched. We were playing charades. Nevertheless, for the architect's sake, we had to appear enthusiastic.

We sat down at his table. He gazed at us over the top of his glasses then rolled out the plans, weighting the corners with the oddments of his craft: a brick, a catalogue of door handles, a stapler, two Bob Dylan CDs.

I stared at the arrangements of oblong shapes that made up the house. What did they mean?

'What's the floor area?' I asked.

'About two hundred and thirty square metres,' he said.

In other words we were truly in the realms of fantasy. The questions were: Do we dream on? Or do something about reality? We opted for a mix – magic realists to the end.

'It's too big,' I said.

'It's got the things you wanted,' he replied. He jabbed a finger at the drawing, pointing out the rooms. 'And there's the platform for Harry.'

Harry was a large and heavy (fifty-plus kilogram) wooden carving of a hippopotamus. We bought him in Zimbabwe at a roadside market outside Harare. He cost me, after lengthy discussions that involved much staring into the middle distance and a round of beers, Z$200, R50 in South African currency, some half a dozen T-shirts, three towels, a torch and batteries, a ballpoint pen, and the shirt off my back.

'But you said we should work on a realistic budget?' I pressed.

'Is this a column next to the stairs? How wonderful,' Jill enthused.

'My words were a "generous budget",' he reminded me. 'How much have you got?'

'A lot less than that thanks to the stock market crash.'

'That's a good pantry,' said Jill.

'You'll find the money,' said the architect.

Once again he gazed at me over the top of his glasses. 'But what do you think of the house?' Up to that moment I hadn't seen the house.

The house, strangely, wasn't a surprise. Somehow the drawings matched the vague house that ghosted in my imagination. As our friend talked us through the plan I kept feeling that I'd been there before. Not that I could see the colour of the walls or the arrangement of our paintings or the furniture but I had a complacent sense of inevitability. Things were going to happen whether I liked it or not, and this house was one of those things.

The design of the house was exactly what we both wanted: long and narrow with a pitched roof, the rafters exposed, the bricks unplastered. The dining room, sitting room and kitchen were open plan. Three French doors with shutters opened from there on to a deck and the view beyond. At the end of this room, up three steps, was our bedroom, and underneath this was my study. The second bedroom was big enough to be comfortable, but not big enough to encourage interminable stays by friends. Most importantly, the house had odd corners and would have unexpected well-framed views of the sea, the mountains, the wetlands, and of a future verdant garden of fynbos and sunbirds. This took no great powers of imagination.

In profile the house reflected not only elements of my history but an open, spacious way of life that we both craved after the claustrophobia of Berlin and Muizenberg. The double storey component recalled colonial settler houses but next to this the deck and French doors were Mediterranean. At the back of the house the steep pitch of the roof flattened over the kitchen and adjacent rooms in a clever adaptation of that essential feature of South African makeshift farm and dorp life, the afdak. In the language of architects the afdak is the 'servant' building to the 'master' building. Not for nothing did our version contain the services: the kitchen, bathrooms, and Jill's office.

'Shall I proceed?' asked the architect.

'Please,' we chorused. Life was unpredictable. Some unknown relative might leave us a large legacy in the next few months.

In the after-gloom of the stock market 'correction' with home mortgage interest rates at twenty-five percent and the property market now completely moribund we decided to sell our house. There was no logic to this decision except that it was summer and a mad blue southeaster was billowing through the rafters. Surely summer was the best time to put a house on the market, although we were not entirely convinced there'd be any response. A neighbour's house down the street had been on the books for eighteen months without so much as an offer. But then she was opposite a brothel and a bar for down-at-heel whites. In addition, the nearby hairdressing salon catering for Africa's refugees wasn't exactly a major drawcard for potential buyers. There were serious reasons other than the 'financial indicators' against her. Even without her immediate drawbacks, however, we were not going to hold our breath. Ours was more a gesture of desperation than strategic planning.

Needless to say the estate agents gushed when they saw our house. Oh, this was so lovely. Oh, they could think of half a dozen people who would love this home. Oh, if anything had a chance of being sold in Muizenberg it was this house.

'How much do you think we should ask for?' I queried.

They – a tall man with a briefcase, and a short man with a gold tooth – looked at one another. Grimaced. Shrugged. Avoided our eyes. Cited a long list of obvious reasons that were not in our favour and then came up with a figure so far below our expectations I was staggered. But, oh, our house was lovely and their estimate wasn't a reflection on either us or the house. And they had some people in mind who they would approach and at that price they might be tempted despite ...

The despite was left drifting. At the sort of figures the agents were talking we would hardly have enough money to dig the foundations of a new house. If we sold our only consolation would be an escape from Muizenberg. But what consolation was this given the extortionate rents being demanded across the city?

'Perhaps you could come in at a slightly higher price and say it was negotiable,' suggested the tall agent with the briefcase.

We named a figure. The agents kept poker-faced.

'It'll be difficult,' said the man with the gold tooth.

'You need to get people to the house,' said his colleague, tapping his fingers on the briefcase. 'If you can entice them in the house will sell itself.'

'We would like sole agency,' said the man with the gold tooth while his colleague shuffled through papers in the briefcase. We acquiesced and then haggled about their commission, bringing them down to a more reasonable percentage.

'You must be absolutely comfortable with the arrangement,' we were told, the gold tooth flashing as we signed a contract giving them sole agency.

The contract disappeared into the briefcase. They stood up. 'Please don't expect miracles,' they said. 'These are hard times.'

As I closed the front door on the estate agents I found myself apologising to the house. I'd betrayed it. Sold out the knots of wood in the Oregon pine boards that I'd lauded over the years for the character they gave the floors. Spurned the rooms that we'd put so much effort and money into decorating. Signed away with a ballpoint pen the renovations, the quirks and corners that had made the house remarkable. Suddenly our loyalty was to an overgrown patch of mountainside with a view down the wind, and that was where we wanted to be. For a snip we were prepared to walk out on a house that had sheltered us for sixteen years. Where I'd written most of my books. Where our beloved cat was buried. What fickleness. Didn't memories mean anything? I cringed at the house's silent rebuke.

A number of weeks passed before we heard from the estate agents again. This was much as we'd expected and it was almost a surprise when, shortly before Christmas, the man with the gold tooth phoned to say he had an interested client, a single woman. Paradoxically, despite Muizenberg's reputation, there were a number of single women in the vicinity. A quick count revealed that on a street of fifteen houses, seven were owned by single women. The signs were positive. Could we dare to hope that against the odds, luck was about to intervene? In response we gave the house a thorough cleaning.

The appointment was for five o'clock on a Saturday afternoon. Saturday afternoon couldn't be regarded as the best time to visit the ghetto, especially if you weren't used to hordes of young men drinking in the streets, the loud noise of their boomboxes, the shrieks of drunken women, and the litter that swirled about these lives. You could take fright when confronted by this outpost of township life, especially if you'd never set foot outside the white suburbs. You might clutch at your handbag and tell the estate agent not to bother stopping, that you'd had second thoughts. Then again, some Saturday afternoons were quiet and uneventful.

At midday on this Saturday I heard the rumble that heralded a street party. I sighed at the grim inevitability: the bastards weren't going to give us a break, they were going to behave badly. Perhaps, I hoped forlornly, they'd be dead drunk by five o'clock. No such luck. By five o'clock the rumble was growing ever louder.

On time the estate agent arrived with the single woman. While we cowered in the study she was whisked through the house in what seemed like less than five minutes. She had no questions, she had no comments, she obviously had more than half an ear cocked to the increasing volume of the voices in the street. And then, as I opened the front door, what sounded like a riot erupted. Suddenly half-dressed men came sprinting down the street, whether chasing or being chased was difficult to tell. Others were shouting. Women were screaming. Of all the strange events I'd witnessed in Muizenberg, such vocal anger was new. The single woman took one look at the men pounding past, and no doubt thinking she'd landed in the midst of a Rwandan massacre, dived into the estate agent's car.

'I can't deal with this,' she screamed. The man with the gold tooth rushed after her uselessly explaining that this was unusual, the refugee problem was being taken care of, there was nothing to be alarmed about, she was perfectly safe. They sped off.

Jill and I were left speechless on the stoep, raging inside with frustrated anger as groups of semi-naked young black men shouted and gesticulated at one another in French. Right outside our house five men were remonstrating with a man who kept trying to shake off their clutches. Farther up the street the scene was being repeated. Unexpectedly the protagonist from this group broke free and, blood smeared across his face, charged at his foe outside our house. There was an uproar. Men lunged after him, caught him, and hauled him back up the road. What looked and sounded like a clash of warring factions was actually the noisy negotiations of a peacekeeping force. What had happened, I imagined, was that at the end of a long day of drinking beer the conflict between a refugee Hutu and a refugee Tutsi was revived and blows exchanged. The violence spilled onto the street.

I stood with a bunch of neighbours watching calm being restored. The refugees ignored us, neither apologised for disturbing the quiet, nor tried to reassure us the violence wouldn't break out among them again. They treated us as they always treated us: with disdain. We didn't exist. That they were a disruption in our neighbourhood caused not a flicker of unease in their consciences. I resented this attitude. I empathised with their desperate situation, but I was infuriated by their part in the destruction of Muizenberg. More particularly I felt helpless: the municipality wouldn't act against the slum landlords who housed the refugees, the police wouldn't stop their excesses. There was nothing to be done but endure or get out. Yet even the second option seemed to rest on the assumption that the conflict in Rwanda or Congo or Sudan could be kept in check for a Saturday afternoon.

Within ten minutes the voluble peace negotiations were over and the street was as quiet as any suburban street late on a Saturday afternoon. If the estate agent had brought his client round just a short while later she would have known nothing of this fracas.

I've always believed this was how it was in times of revolution: if you were one street away from the action you wouldn't know it was happening.

Our initial reaction to this intervention in our efforts to escape Muizenberg was anger. We swore and cursed and raged within the privacy of our house. We had a drink to restore our sanity.

'I can't believe it,' Jill kept saying. 'I just can't believe they did this.'

'But did you see how she dived into the car?'

'She was terrified.'

Which was when we saw the funny side and couldn't help but laugh. After all the timing was perfect. As exact as the crash of the Asian Tiger stock markets.

9: *A More Exact Sense Of Place*

As a welcome distraction from our frustrations, during early summer I was commissioned to write a series of articles on the émigré groups that, over the city's three centuries, had made Cape Town what it was.

Of course the assignment was more than a distraction: it was an opportunity to examine some of the families who had woven their lives into the history of the city. And after years of living too lightly in Cape Town I felt a need to 'get under its skin'.

The series formed part of a campaign initiated by the editor of the *Cape Times* in response to what he saw as a fractured city.

Five months earlier, in August 1998, a bomb had exploded in Planet Hollywood, a popular Waterfront restaurant, killing two and causing life-altering injuries to five others, including two children who lost limbs. Initially the blast was linked to recent bombings in Nairobi and Dar-es-Salaam and widely believed to be the work of Muslim fundamentalists. Such speculation was enough to expose the racial and racist vitriol that for the most part ran hidden through the city like its sewers.

'Readers have sent in letters of such irrational hatred that we couldn't print them,' the editor told me. 'I was horrified at the levels of intolerance.'

In an attempt to understand the city he wanted to run a campaign under the banner One City, Many Cultures that would reveal the diversity of the groups in Cape Town and lead, he hoped, to at least a respect for the different beliefs and rituals. 'Would you write on names?' he asked. 'Names as indications of where people came from to find a new life in Cape Town.' Or were brought from as slaves. I could think of no better way to pass the summer. Besides, as Berlin was making me look again at Cape Town, this would help to establish a more exact sense of place for myself.

During the founding decades Cape Town didn't really have a name. Table Mountain was known to the Khoi as Hoerikwaggo – the Sea-Mountain – but European sailors and settlers referred to it as de Kaapsche Vlek (the Cape settlement) or Cabo (the Cape). By the mid-eighteenth century locals and visitors were beginning to call the rapidly growing 'settlement' Kaapstad, the Cape Town, and this was the name that gradually cohered. The point was that Cape Town's name evolved: the city was named by its inhabitants over generations, no one, no committee, sat down and unilaterally conferred a name. There wasn't even a plebiscite, it simply came about.

Today, while no one is inclined to rename the city, there is every intention of renaming some of its streets – an indication, if ever one were needed, of a city struggling to imagine itself.

This was why in 1998 Joe Marks, paramount chief of the Outeniqua tribe and a then Democratic Party Member of Parliament, applied to have the name of Adderley Street changed to Eyamma Boulevard. His request was turned down by the city council, who offered a compromise: when next they had a street to name they would use his suggestion. Marks was, and remains, outraged and disappointed. 'Either we use this name for Adderley Street or it's not used at all,' he argued. 'It certainly cannot be wasted on some little by-road. For me this was a chance for the city fathers to make a significant gesture by honouring one of the founding heroes of South Africa.'

Marks's strong feelings and the story behind his suggestion had a long tap root. For him a name was not simply a name, it was an identity – a sense of place. According to Marks, the oral history of his people told of how Eyamma was dispatched as the leader of seventeen fighters to harass the Europeans with the intention of forcing the Dutch East India Company to abandon their newly established settlement and flee the Cape. Eyamma subsequently engaged in hit-and-run operations against the settlers but was eventually caught and imprisoned with Autshumao – known to the Dutch as Harry the Strandloper – on Robben Island, the Island's first political prisoners.

Eyamma subsequently escaped and continued his campaign of

attrition, was recaptured, reincarcerated on the Island, and once again escaped. When he was next captured, in the area of Mowbray, his kneecaps were smashed and he was pierced through the stomach with a steel rod. Some days later – Marks had it – he died of his wounds with the words: 'It is better to die for an idea that will live, than to live for an idea that will die.'

'I feel that as Eyamma was one of the first political opponents of colonialism, he should be remembered in Cape Town's main street,' Marks insisted.

Marks chose a street that had already had its name changed once for political reasons. During the Dutch years the settlement established itself around two streams that ran through its vegetable gardens to the sea. The paths became a street with houses on either side and this was named the Heerengracht, after the Herengracht in Amsterdam.

Even when the British finally took the Cape as a colonial possession in 1814, the Heerengracht retained its name for another twenty-five years before being renamed Adderley Street in honour of Charles Bowyer Adderley. Adderley never seemed to have visited the Cape but as a member of the British parliament he campaigned strongly against sending convicts to the Cape Colony in 1848. Out of gratitude the city of Cape Town thanked him by renaming the Heerengracht in 1850.

The Heerengracht's story, however, didn't end there. When the new docks were built in the 1950s and the foreshore reclamation gave additional land to the city, the extension to Adderley Street was named the Heerengracht.

The business of naming and renaming is fraught with political agendas. The bottom of Adderley Street being a case in point. When the streets of the foreshore – Hans Strydom, Hertzog Boulevard, Coen Steytler, D F Malan, Oswald Pirow – were named the Nationalist Party had recently come to power and they were clearly making an attempt to lay claims to an historical authority both in terms of the recent and the distant past.

A scant fifty years later those names might well be struck from the kerbstones and the street maps as Cape Town undergoes a symbolic change. Of course symbolic changes – which could be regarded as merely cosmetic – nevertheless have an uncanny way of rousing public feeling. To some, street names are the markers of pain and suffering and should be changed, to others they are the recorders of history. Which may be why Klipfontein Road, where the coloured community fought running battles with the police in the eighties, should not be renamed Dr Nelson Mandela Drive as was once proposed. The memories of what many saw as a heroic time didn't belong to Dr Nelson Mandela Drive, they belonged to Klipfontein Road. What would be lost with the name change? To make the matter more complex the Muslim hawkers in the street were adamant that if the name were to be changed then it should rather be called after Imam Shaheed Haroen who died in detention in 1969. Such were their convictions that in November 1998 they held a meeting to symbolically rename the road.

Although names carry social or political weight at the moment they are conferred and for some time afterwards, inevitably this is soon forgotten. To many, Queen Victoria Street may need no explanation, but who – except the politically sensitive – remembers Oswald Pirow let alone his fascist tendencies and his admiration for Hitler? Who would know that Sir Charles Henry Darling, lieutenant governor at the Cape from 1852 to 1855, gave his name to Darling Street? Or that Sir Lowry's Road was named after Sir Lowry Cole, the British governor here between 1828 and 1833? Similarly, judging by snap street polls, there are many young people in Guguletu who don't know that the initials of the 'NY' streets stand for 'native yard'.

But the point is not what lingers or doesn't linger in the public memory, the point is that street names, even when they are purely descriptive such as Strand, Buitenkant, Buitengracht, Long, or Bree, carry reminders from the past. And those reminders give a city its historical resonance. In fact they tell the city's story, an argument for keeping even the names that rankle.

As a port city there is every reason to retain the geographically descriptive name, Cape Town, although some believe it is not African enough. Yet, in common with all port cities, a major part of Cape Town's history is about accepting immigrants and refugees, about taking in strangers. In other words about people who come here to begin new lives, either because they have been enticed by glowing accounts, or because they are fleeing from wars or poverty.

Often – usually – the immigrants were not welcomed and were treated harshly. Frequently, the newcomers behaved equally badly. It is striking that the comments about the degradation, poverty, crime, wild sexual orgies and drunkenness of the inhabitants of Irish Town in the 1830s – the area around Plein Street and Constitution Hill – are not dissimilar to the letters in today's newspapers decrying the Congolese, Nigerians, and Angolans seeking a haven in parts of Cape Town, and my own experience in Muizenberg. Perhaps as the rowdy inhabitants of Irish Town were absorbed or had dispersed by the late 1840s, the same process will work on the new immigrants.

Perhaps this is how it always has been. The Khoi pastoralists were wiped out or assimilated. For the slaves brought in during the next two hundred and seventy years Cape Town must have been a place of great unhappiness. For those born here in captivity life was hard. Today those pains are hardly remembered. Just as Cape Town's other scars are now often sites of curiosity – the dungeons at the Castle, the kramat on Signal Hill, the Slave Lodge. And whoever pauses to think of the meaning of Gallows Hill where men were hung drawn and quartered in public? Or that the Company Gardens symbolises the start of Cape Town as a place of sustenance and nourishment?

The broad sweep of Cape Town's history can be seen as a series of immigrations – of which the central African refugees/emigrants are merely the latest. Between 1652 and the 1870s there was a constant influx of Dutch, German and English. Simultaneously people were being brought as slaves from Angola, Madagascar, Mozambique, China, India, Indonesia. To the indigenous Khoi pastoralists who used the mountain bowl to graze their sheep and cattle in summer, the arrival of these newcomers meant, eventually and bitterly, the end of their nation as they were wiped out or assimilated through intermarriage. From the 1880s to the 1900s came significant numbers of Jews from Eastern Europe – some escaping poverty and pogroms, others drawn by the discovery of diamonds and gold. According to a census in 1891 the Jewish community numbered a thousand, by

1904 that figure had risen to eight thousand. Adding to the mixture was an Indian community six hundred strong by 1899, although 'Indian corner stores' were already a feature of the city in the 1880s.

The essence of Cape Town, I felt, was that of a cosmopolitan city and if any one book confirmed this, while simultaneously offering clues to the recorded and the secret life of Cape Town, it was that useful but humble publication the latest telephone directory. Here were not only the names of the current city but also of historic Cape Town. I decided to base my research on a completely haphazard series of choices.

For instance, sprinkled around the city were a number of blocks of flats called Arderne Courts or Arderne Mansions and in the suburb of Claremont there was an Arderne Gardens. Who, I wondered, was this Arderne? The telephone book listed only four Ardernes, relatively few given the seeming importance of the name. I chose to start with Richard Arderne for no particular reason other than his was the last name on the list. His address was the extremely expensive seaside suburb of Llandudno.

A few days later I was sitting in the cool white upstairs lounge of his house with a view of the sea that filled the front window. The morning was crystalline; the sea azure. From somewhere came the squeals and laughter of children playing. Richard didn't know much about his family's past except that a forebear had emigrated from England in the 1830s. However some proud relative had published a history and he lent me a copy. This book provided most of the information I needed.

Since the 1840s the Ardernes had been a solid well-educated middle-class family with strong church connections. Their founder, Ralph Henry Arderne, bequeathed his garden at Claremont to the city as a park, and although the family never achieved great wealth or sought political office they were professional people with a hand in Cape Town's commercial affairs. Nothing particularly noteworthy: the Ardernes were a respectable family. Except that one of the four Ardernes listed in the telephone book lived in the coloured suburb of Grassy Park. Here I sensed a Cape Town story of love across the colour bar waiting to be told. I have always been fascinated by these stories because they speak of human emotions that defied family prejudice and social conventions. (For most of the last fifty years they also defied the law.)

Since the marriage of Krotoa, the daughter of a Cochoqua chief, to Pieter van Meerhof less than ten years after the Dutch established their settlement at the Cape, the city's love story has paid scant attention to skin colour. And yet lodged deep in the hearts of so many coloured people is a sense of shame that the relationships that produced them are somehow illegitimate.

As I suspected, Godfrey Arderne of Grassy Park was related to Richard Arderne of Llandudno in that loose and mysterious way that connected so many families in Cape Town: shared name, inexact history. He regarded Ralph Henry Arderne as a forebear yet how his lineage tied in was not to be found in the genealogy given at the back of the book on the Arderne's history.

Essentially this didn't matter. Essentially Godfrey Arderne's family tree was part of a major theme in the city's history: the creation of a population that regarded Cape Town as home but could trace bloodlines to Europe, India, Indonesia, southern, western and eastern Africa, Madagascar, China. What did matter, I felt, was the pride Godfrey Arderne took in his family origins.

His house was in a quiet close. Here he lived with his wife and youngest daughter, and the family of a married daughter. He invited me into his small neat lounge and we talked while elsewhere the family happily prepared to attend a wedding. He spoke about his life and his career as a fitter and turner. In a few years he would retire and devote himself to painting water colours. I asked him about his grandparents.

'My grandfather was Henry John Arderne who married Martha,' he recounted, and then paused. I waited. He stared at the pattern on the carpet. 'I don't know anything about her,' he said. 'Nobody in the family knows who she was or where she came from. We don't even know what her surname was. All we know is that she must have been black or coloured.'

He then told me a sad story about Henry and Martha that split the family and said something of the nature of the shame that only the new generations will not know. Shortly after their marriage Henry took his young wife to meet members of the family living in Sea

Point. Imagine him knocking on the front door. The door being opened by a relative who says: 'Look, Henry, we're pleased to see you, but do you think you can ask your good wife to go round to the back door. You know how it is …' Martha knew very well how it was. Humiliated and angry she vowed never to see them again.

Godfrey told this brief anecdote dispassionately until a thought struck him: 'You know,' he reflected, 'this was before apartheid. This must have been in the nineteenth century because my father was born in 1900.' He made no further comment but shook his head. I let the silence lengthen. He glanced at me. 'So it wasn't just apartheid that separated everybody.'

I asked him what it was like seeing his surname on buildings and at the entrance to the Arderne Gardens in Claremont? He paused for a long time, his eyes fixed on the opposite wall. Then he said, 'I went to walk in the Arderne Gardens the other day. I wanted to walk where my great grandfather walked, and I don't care what the other side of the family say but I felt proud about my family heritage. When my elder son was married he had his wedding photographs taken in those gardens. I think there is a lot of significance to our name.'

Because of Martha's story, I thought so too.

One of the distinguishing features of the Cape Town telephone directory is the long lists of 'month' names – as clear an indication as any of the city's slave legacy. Slave owners frequently named slaves after classical Greek or Roman gods, or after Old Testament figures, or conferred facetious names like Fortuijn (fortune) or Pattat (sweet potato) or Slim (clever), but once their classical learning was exhausted slave owners fell back on the names of the months. Which might also explain the origins of a catchy but seemingly meaningless ditty that simply reels off the months of the year as its lyrics. Some historians have suggested that oceanic slave traders, auctioning large lots of slaves at the quayside, resorted to the months as a handy naming mechanism. And the song came about as the slaves' ironic way of dealing with their arbitrary names.

One of the most famous 'month' names in Cape Town is that of the mountaineer, Dr Ed February. To my query about his family origins he responded with due irony: 'I'm sure we came from slaves, it's a proud tradition in this city' – then he refered me to his cousin, Paul February, who he said, had 'traced back the family to a freed slave who had a farm in the Stellenbosch area.'

I phoned Paul February. He was only too happy to talk about what he knew of the family's lineage but couldn't, irrefutably, make the final connection. This clearly irritated him a good deal as he wanted to claim the freed, farm-owning slave as a forebear.

'All I can tell you is that I remember my father talking about an Oom Willie who was a freed slave,' he told me. 'My father had no problems with this but other members of my family wouldn't have anything to do with such a probability. Any rate my father believed that his forebear was a freed slave who was given a farm, Kleinvlei, on being set free. But there's no piece of paper to prove that we are actually descended from this man. You know how it is: there are very few records, mostly no records, for people who weren't white.'

Then Paul February asked if I knew why there were a lot of Januarys in the telephone book but only a few Decembers? I said I didn't. 'Let me tell you,' he said. 'There is a story that slaves were often given the names of the months in which they were freed. Well, no slave owner was going to free slaves in December because then he'd have no one to wash up the Christmas dishes.' And Paul February laughed and laughed.

Slaves weren't the Dutch East India Company's only human 'import' into Cape Town. Political dissidents were another. Fortuitously for the Company's governors at the Cape, Table Bay had an island – Robben Island – that could be used as a prison. It was far enough offshore to deter anyone with thoughts of swimming through the cold waters to freedom, but within a few hours' sail of the town. Here were banished both rebellious locals and those suspected of fomenting insurrection in the Company's eastern colonies. One of these was a troublesome prince exiled in the 1770s to Robben Island from the island of Tidore in the Indonesian archipelago. He was accused of conspiring with the British against the Dutch. The man's name was Abdullah ibn Qadi Abd al-Salam, although he later became known as Tuan Guru, which literally means Master Teacher. While incarcerated on the island the prince wrote two books stressing the acceptance by faith of Allah's will in the world – a doctrine ideally suited to the lives of exiles and slaves. These works were to form the basis of Cape Islam and Tuan Guru was to become its first dedicated exponent. After his release in 1792 the teacher established a religious school at his house in Dorp Street.

Prior to Tuan Guru's arrival at the town a small Islamic community of slaves, exiles and free-blacks (a description that applied to manumitted slaves) had started to form in the late years of the Dutch East India Company's rule. While the Dutch didn't encourage Islam, they didn't suppress it either and this growing tolerance allowed the community to establish itself. By the 1790s regular Friday prayers were being conducted in the stone quarries at the foot of Signal Hill.

After the first British invasion of the Cape in 1795, permission was given for a warehouse in Dorp Street to be converted into the Auwal Mosque with Tuan Guru as imam. Then under the short-lived Batavian government the Dutch guaranteed religious freedom and simultaneously co-opted the growing number of Muslims into a special artillery unit to defend the Cape should the British invade again. When this happened in 1806 at the Battle of Blouberg, Tuan Guru was reputed to have led the Muslim contingent against his former political allies. According to his descendant, Irefaan Rakiep, Tuan Guru's weapons were a sword and shield. Together with the texts written on Robben Island these weapons were now among Rakiep's heirlooms.

Irefaan Rakiep was the highlight of my assignment on the names of Cape Town. It took five weeks and five phone calls before he would agree to see me and even then he was wary. 'People have written so much rubbish about me,' he said during the fourth phone call. 'They think I am lying. Some historians don't believe Tuan Guru founded Islam in Cape Town but I'm telling you they are wrong. He is my ancestor. I have his sword and shield. Without him there would be no Islam in Cape Town. I have his books.' Our conversation – or rather his outburst – ended inconclusively as the others had done. He wanted to think about it. A week later I called again. He was still wavering.

'Why won't you see me?' I asked. 'I'm not interested in what the historians have to say, I want your story in your words.'

He thought about this, and relented. 'Ok, but you're not to write rubbish. You just write what I tell you.'

We agreed to meet a few days later.

Irefaan Rakiep lives in the quiet, ludicrously named Snowdrop Square in Bridgetown. All the streets in the area are named after flowers, an attempt by the town planners of the sixties to give an air of garden tranquillity to an apartheid development. For many of the people who live here were 'invited' to move from District Six.

While I parked in front of his small house he came out to stand stiffly at his garden gate as if he were standing to attention. He wore a tie and a white shirt, a short-sleeved cardigan, brown slacks, well-polished brown shoes. We shook hands. 'Come inside,' he said. He was distant and suspicious and I wondered if I'd made the right decision in pushing him for the interview.

We sat in his front room. Cards wishing him well over Ramadan hung behind the couch. Photographs of his children were arrayed on some cluttered shelves where three plaques honoured his family. Sticky-taped to a wall were posters showing Robben Island from the air and behind it Cape Town and Table Mountain. On another wall were photographs of journalists who had interviewed him and dignitaries he'd met on his trips back to Tidore to visit his forebear's country. Pasted up elsewhere in the lounge was a photostat of the title page of a paper he'd written on Tuan Guru and next to this an injunction from the Sultan of Ternate declaring that 'Haj Nurul Erfan Rakieb is a true descendant from Prince Abdulla from Tidore, Indonesia, who was exiled to Cape Town in South Africa in the year 1770. It is self explanatory that Haj Nurul Erfan is a Prince. He should be addressed as Prince Haj Nurul Erfan Rakieb.'

Rakiep took a card from a dish beside the plaques and handed it to me. 'Do you see this: the people in Java have made me an honorary member of the Malaysian Historical Society and the Indonesian Moslem Intellectual Society. I was the first Cape Malay they had ever seen. When I went back there I said you are my people and they greeted me and confirmed I was a prince.

'Long ago I can remember my father telling me and my brothers that we were princes. And the old people always used to say here come the little princes when we walked into a room. But I only began researching the family history in 1978 and after that I made contacts in Indonesia who helped me establish the facts. So when I went there in 1993 I was welcomed to the royal family of Ternate and Tidore islands as a returning prince.' He stared at me, while I hastily made notes. Then he said, 'Please, come with me I want to show you a video.'

We went through to a small dusty backroom that was dominated by a wardrobe, a ladder, a gas heater, chairs: in the midst of this stack of furniture stood a big screen television and perched on it an old video recorder. He indicated that I should sit on the bed. 'You must excuse the mess,' he apologised, 'since my wife died there is no woman in the house any more.' He started the video and we saw a high mountain under cloud and on the sea a scattering of white boats sailing towards the camera.

'That is me on the royal boat,' he said. The camera turned on the welcoming party and their banners. 'There is a cousin of mine. There is another cousin' – he pointed at some figures. 'It was very hot but I could manage the heat.' We watched the boats pull against a jetty and arms reached out and helped Rakiep disembark. He stood and looked at the people and the mountain, and began praying.

'I said a prayer first taught to Malays at Cape Town by Tuan Guru,' he explained. 'It begins: "Open the doors of goodness and mercy and of sustenance and blessing and of peace."' As he said this Irefaan Rakiep rubbed a handkerchief at his eyes and blew his nose. On the screen he was being ushered towards a motor cavalcade that would drive him through the island's villages.

With a sob he said, 'You see there, my dreams had come true. I went back to the island that my forebear Tuan Guru was banished from.' There was triumph in the choked voice: a sense of accomplishment, as if the hardships the Rakieps had endured over the last two centuries had been vindicated.

Irefaan Rakiep was born in 1922 in District Six. His father was a tailor who worked from home, and at a young age Rakiep would go around town collecting garments for repair. 'District Six was a brotherhood in those days,' he reminisced. 'We were a closed community. Of course we had to struggle for ourselves but we did alright.'

Hidden in this last phrase was a hard story. 'My grandfather,' recounted Rakiep, 'was a very poor man so when my father was young he had to go to Roggebaai and sell koeksisters at the pier. He was barefoot and had only a thin little shirt. At the age of nine or ten my grandmother took him to a Jew who trained him as a tailor. But he had no education, and he always wanted me to have an education.

'I went to Penny School in St Philip Street and then to Gordons School until Standard Two. I wanted to be a doctor but my father couldn't keep me in school so I was sent to a Jew in Hanover Street who taught me to be a tailor. In 1939 at the start of the war there was very little work but I was lucky to get a job with a German Jew in Mill Street. He couldn't speak English so I had to learn a bit of German. I worked for him for a year or so then I went to the factories and finally in 1947 – the year I was married – I opened my own business at home in Hanover Street.'

From District Six the Rakieps moved to Bridgetown. 'We all knew District Six was going to be knocked down so we thought it was best to move rather than wait for the bulldozers,' explained Rakiep. 'But when we came here this place was in the middle of the bush. No electricity. Nothing. Just bush. It was very difficult picking up our lives after the District where there were always friends nearby and you could go for a walk into the town.'

Picking up their lives meant that while Rakiep's wife, Fatima, worked at home as a dressmaker, he found a job as a tailor in Wellington, sixty kilometres away. He would spend the week there, returning on the weekend. During the next twenty years, until Fatima's death in 1972, the couple raised five sons and three daughters.

'At least we could give them an education,' said Rakiep. Suddenly, inexplicably, he rose from his chair and paced the room. His face was contorted with anger and I thought he was going to attack me. Then he pulled out his handkerchief and sat down, weeping. Uselessly I asked if he was alright. If I could get him some water. He looked up and smiled. There was no trace of the previous anguish on his face. 'I am fine now,' he said. 'You see I couldn't have an education. I had to work from when I was very young. But now two of my children are teachers, two became secretaries, one is a television technician.' Then, in what now seems a non sequitur but sounded perfectly logical while he spoke, he said, 'When I met the Sultan of Ternate I told him I was walking under destiny in finding the birthplace of Tuan Guru. But destiny has always led my family. We have had hard times but if you live a pure life then God will help you.'

He wanted me to watch the video again. I made excuses and he said, 'Perhaps another time.' We shook hands. 'You must write a good article,' he added. 'This is a great story. It will make you very famous.'

When I drove away he was again standing to attention at his gate. Or perhaps that was his idea of regal formality, a part of his inheritance.

The stories of Godfrey Arderne, Paul February and Irefaan Rakiep were, by the nature of the assignment, mere glimpses into Cape Town's secret life. But they were enough to endear the place to me all over again. I realised, with some surprise at the adamant nature of my feelings, that I didn't want to live anywhere else. This was the landscape I wanted and although one could do nothing but accept history, I thought it was a story well worth the telling. Cape Town was different. It was unlike any other city in South Africa. Many times I'd heard black people criticise it for not being an 'African' city. Many times I'd heard tourists comment that it felt European. Cape Town was neither African nor European and would remain a hybrid, a city made up of people whose forebears came from elsewhere. Which also applied to the Africans who had settled here.

While the African influence on Cape Town has been more marked in the last twenty years with the collapse of apartheid legislation than at any other period in the city's history, there had always been a small black community. In 1899 it was estimated at ten thousand and itself reflected the diversity that characterised the rest of the city's population. At a baptism on Christmas Eve, 1890, there were three Xhosa speakers, three 'Shangaans', one 'Inhambane', one Zulu, and one Mosotho attending the service.

Since the breakdown of the apartheid laws in the mid-eighties – particularly the Influx Control Act which kept Cape Town as a coloured labour preference area and excluded blacks from getting work here –

Cape Town has acquired more of an 'African' feel. Over a million people now live in the township of Khayelitsha and it is said to swell by ten thousand 'émigrés' from the rural areas of the Eastern Cape each month.

One of these relative 'newcomers' is a man called Maxwell Flekisi who lives with his wife and three children in a self-built brick house in Site C, Khayelitsha. I had never been to Site C before but the moment I drove into the ramshackle warren of brick houses with their lean-tos of corrugated iron packed along narrow concrete streets, a familiar feeling that is a mixture of dread and despondency welled up. Over the last twenty-five years I have experienced it every time I visited a township. Then again, my experience of townships has always been of zones under siege, or where people have recounted to me the grim and harrowing details of their lives. Now I steered carefully along Site C's roads littered with bricks and tyres and broken cars and could not see these places existing in any other way. The poverty was too grinding, the lives, mostly, too exhausted. Yet here and there were garden patches, flowers, tomato bushes, loquat trees. Here and there houses were brightly painted. And like a spider web running over fences, across the roads, trailing through the gutters were the electric wires that linked those houses with electricity to those without.

I stopped outside Flekisi's home and could not imagine life here: the early morning sounds, the hot days of wind, the long hours of Sunday afternoons. Or rather I did not want to imagine this life.

As I drove up Maxwell Flekisi was throwing out seed for the pigeons that nested in a coop outside his front door. The birds came flocking and he scattered more seed among them and into their nesting boxes. 'I love these birds,' he said while we stood watching them. 'But they cost a lot of money to feed.'

The birds pecked furiously at the corn about his feet. He sighed and glanced at me: 'You come to ask me about my home. This isn't my home. Transkei is my home but I have got to come here to get money. There are no jobs or money in Transkei so I am just staying here to earn money and then when I am old and the children are grown up I will go home.'

Flekisi earned a living as a petrol jockey at a Muizenberg service station which was where we'd met, and during our short forecourt conversations I learnt that his pay was low and that his financial worries consumed him.

'Sometimes at night I wake up with this big pain in my head like it is going to explode with all this worry,' he told me. 'I don't know what to do. There is nothing I can do. I can only pray to God.'

As an archbishop in the Zionist Christian Church, Flekisi was not expressing himself lightly. His faith ran deep and yet it was undercut by a fundamental despair. When he put his weekly wage of R193 on the kitchen table he never knew if it was going to see his family through seven days. 'You know what it is,' he said, 'food is expensive. It costs more to feed the baby than for us. And these days the children want many things, new jeans, new shoes, and not any shoes, they must have the right name. How is this money going to buy these things?'

The question was one he came back to again and again because since the 1994 elections Flekisi had felt an increasing edge of desperation in his life. A desperation that rendered all the freedoms and dignity guaranteed by the new political dispensation void. 'I can say that the promises that were made by the ANC have not been kept,' he declared. 'I can say things are much worse now than they have ever been. What does having freedom mean if you have no money?

'Perhaps for my children it will be better because they will have more education. That is the thing that I can hope for. That maybe for them and my grandchildren they will not have to struggle to find money.' Yet even this thought clouded his face. 'This year, my daughter, Vuyakazi, is in matric but matric is not enough anymore. When she is finished the school she must study at college or maybe university and this costs much money. But if she does not have those papers then how will she find a job? Everybody has these papers now.'

We were sitting in his tiny front room that was dominated by a large settee and a television. In a corner hung a poster of the smiling Archbishop Flekisi and taped next to this an alpine snow scene that had probably been cut from a calendar. While Flekisi talked his baby daughter crawled about his knees and squirmed on his lap.

Cape Town for Maxwell Flekisi had never been, and never would be, a place he would remember with fondness, let alone call home. Since he started seeking work in the city in 1975 when pass laws and acts such as Influx Control and Urban Areas and the Coloured Labour Preference Policy meant that his movements were restricted and his options limited, Cape Town had been an ordeal. A city he endured in much the way slaves might once have suffered it. But while slaves were brought here by force, Flekisi came of his own accord but equally unwillingly.

'I was born at Kcala near Lady Frere,' he recounted. 'When I passed Standard Seven there was no more money for me to go to school and the family needed me to start earning a living. At that time my father was already working in Cape Town as a petrol pump attendant. So I said I will go to Cape Town.

'In those days you had to get a permit which meant you could work in Cape Town for one year and then you had to go home again and the next year you must get another permit. So I came to Cape Town and for many months I sold fruit and vegetables and chickens beside the road. But my father showed me how to be a petrol pump attendant and eventually I got one of those jobs.

'All this time I was living in shacks at Nyanga Bush, Browns Farm, Guguletu, Crossroads. My last place was in Crossroads, 1985. But this was too difficult. Every day you come home and you do not know if your house is bulldozed or burnt in the fighting. [At the time Crossroads was the scene of pitched battles as the apartheid order sought to shore up its crumbling authority.] You do not know if your wife and child are safe. So that is when we moved here to Khayelitsha.'

While Maxwell told this story, his wife, Eunice, sat to one side on a wooden stool gazing out the window. Before I could ask how she came to Cape Town she got up and disappeared into another room. 'She also came from Transkei to find work,' Maxwell explained on her behalf and sketched an experience that resembled his own: casual work as a domestic, squatting in makeshift shacks, harassment by officials and the police. He picked up his daughter. 'I look forward to going back to Transkei,' he said. 'This Cape Town is my children's place but it is not mine.'

As I drove out of Site C – another of those created townships where 'surplus people' were invited and enticed to settle in an attempt to prevent the squatter settlements nearer the city growing too big – my mood of dread and despondency did not lift. I turned on to the coast road that skirts False Bay: the ocean glistened in the late afternoon sunlight and the peninsula's mountain chain was barely visible through the white haze. The beauty did nothing to ease my thoughts. Like Maxwell Flekisi I hoped his children would have things easier.

10: *Double Espressos At Panini's*

Late in January 1999 the estate agent telephoned to say he had clients who were interested in our house. They were holidaying in Muizenberg, in fact just down the street behind the émigrés, and they were charmed by the village and thought our house frontage looked cute. Could they come round tomorrow morning at nine o'clock?

'These are very nice people,' he said. 'They are from New York. He is an eccentric man. I know he will like your house.'

I wasn't sure how to interpret this but the agent sounded excited. Clearly in his scheme of things only the truly odd would give Muizenberg a second glance. I thought he was probably right. Anyone who had spent three weeks on holiday here, and near the endless noise of the émigrés, had to be more concerned about a dream than the reality.

Since the single woman and the incident of the feverish Rwandans there had been not so much as a tentative enquiry about our house. Of course this was to be expected but the total lack of interest was also disconcerting. Especially as we were emotionally ready for a change. Which meant we had to guard against frustration and despondency, particularly as the all-too-frequent incidents that bedevilled the neighbourhood were becoming increasingly difficult to handle.

On Christmas Day alone we had repeatedly been pulled from the quiet of our house by shouting and howls in the street. On three occasions we'd prevented couples from inflicting violence on one another. The last disturbance had also brought out John, a relatively new neighbour in an adjacent street. An imposing man and unafraid to intervene physically, he had quickly separated the warring couple. Once they had staggered off we stood talking with him and learnt that he had left a rough coloured region of Retreat in the hopes of finding a more settled middle-class neighbourhood. He laughed good naturedly at the inappropriateness of his move. 'I'm sure Muizenberg will improve,' he said, adding: 'If there's any more trouble call me. These people won't listen to you whiteys but they'll pay attention to me.'

When the prospective buyers arrived at nine o'clock and I opened the door I knew they would buy the house. The agent introduced us and I stood back to let them in. They were an affable, urbane couple and went slowly but with growing enthusiasm through the house. They saw the walls of bookshelves in the study and immediately spoke about sitting there quietly to think and write. They asked about our paintings and photographs, they admired the Oregon pine floors, were entranced by the deep plum colour of our bedroom and the elegant pink of the sitting room walls. They wanted to know when the house was built and who had owned it and how long we'd stayed there? We showed them photographs of the house when we'd moved in and the stages of renovation. They took one look at the small brick-paved back yard with the bougainvillaea in full scarlet and hawk-moths at the lavender and spoke of peaceful breakfasts where they could glance up and see the mountain in early sun. I marvelled at the difference in our Muizenbergs. The one they talked about was one we'd had but it was no longer like that for us nor could ever be again. They went back inside the house inquiring about any problems and whether there was rising damp. They wanted to know what light fittings we were taking and if we'd consider leaving any of the blinds. We talked generally about our lives and I learnt that he had old roots in Muizenberg and that as they were moving into a more leisurely time in their lives they wanted a retreat, somewhere they could spend the northern winter. They asked about our plans for the future and how long we thought it would take to build in Glencairn. After an hour and a half they left. As the front door closed Jill said, 'They're going to put in an offer. They've practically moved in already.' I had to agree with her. But could we trust our luck? Certainly I couldn't imagine our house being bought by nicer people. My betrayal seemed less odious. The house would still be loved.

That afternoon the agents came round with an offer. It was for a lot less than our asking price but this was a cash deal and, most importantly, they offered a year's free accommodation while our new house was built. I couldn't believe our good fortune. On a simple sale like this transfer would take about six weeks. By March we would have the money in the bank. And we'd escaped the trauma of moving to rented accommodation. This alone was worth thousands of rands. I had dreaded the thought of the disruption: temporary phone numbers, temporary addresses, living out of boxes for ten to twelve months. A nightmare. I stared into the blue and asked in grateful bewilderment: Why us, Lord? Why us? As usual there was no answer, merely cosmic indifference. But it had never seemed so benign before.

We accepted the offer without haggling. Suddenly what we'd longed for was a reality. More to the point we had twelve months to finalise the house plans, submit them to the local council for approval, contract a builder, and build. And as Jill was talking about being in the new house by Christmas or the New Year at the latest the real deadline was only ten months away. I phoned some builders. One needed to start immediately, another said he didn't touch anything on the side of a mountain, a third said June or July would be early enough. A fourth asked if the plans were approved. I said they weren't even ready. He whistled softly, one of those chill little whistles that suggests you have a fundamental flaw in your understanding of how the world works. He advised me to submit the plans immediately. He said sometimes approval could take almost two months. Depending on how the officials were feeling. I became alarmed. I phoned the architect.

In the meantime I had to apply my mind to some serious financial strategising. The sale of the house would pay off the plot and leave a healthy balance that would at least get the building to roof height assuming there weren't any nasty surprises during the foundation stage. The question was how did I get from there to a finished house?

I'd gambled with my life before but I'd been thirty then, and the changes I'd forced weren't so much a gamble as a desperate desire for a different lifestyle. At forty-seven the stakes were higher but was there an option? And wouldn't it be interesting to see how things panned out? So in the deep dark hours of a February night, as I lay petrified with fear about the future, I decided to cash in my pension investments.

The transfer should have gone through without any problems. Should have. But because I trusted professional people – like lawyers – to do their job I tended not to chase them. This was a fundamental mistake. Because nobody does anything until coerced. Despite a whole new genre of non-fiction devoted entirely and endlessly to the subject of business management, and how efficiency, some thought and client care will make a business successful the basic philosophy was still: respond to pressure, nothing else is important enough. This, although it took six weeks to realise it, was the business practice adopted by our conveyancing lawyers. When I phoned to ask if the transfer was through I was told: We've got a little problem and it's taking the municipality a while to sort out the matter. I learnt that the problem had brought the process to a halt five weeks previously. And that despite two subsequent phone calls from the lawyers to the municipality there'd been no progress. Not that I thought two phone calls were an indication of any serious intention to resolve the issue.

The problem was this: the municipality wanted the new buyers to sign a waiver granting them permission to demolish a back wall should they ever need to because said wall was built over the municipal sewage pipes. The buyers were understandably reluctant to do this. Worse: they were beginning to feel that if we'd not disclosed this what else had we kept hidden?

I explained to the lawyer that we'd never signed such a waiver. I also suggested that he fax me the relevant municipal documents. Which he did and the problem was instantly obvious: the erf number was right but the address was in the nearby suburb of Lakeside.

Yet no one in either the lawyer's office or the municipality had paused to question this discrepancy. Half an hour later a blushing municipal official confessed that a dyslexic typist had transposed two digits in the erf number of the Lakeside house. And because municipalities and lawyers were fixated on the truth of erf numbers they paid no attention to such frivolously poetic devices as street names and numbers. I had lost a month's interest. In material terms this would have bought a toilet, basin and taps. Had the lawyer apologised? Had the lawyer rebated his fees for this extraordinary incompetency? To both questions the answer was no.

While the lawyers wallowed in their inadequacy the architect finalised the plans. These sessions were sometimes difficult because compromises between his design and what we wanted had to be made. I came to understand that architects didn't have it easy. Their creativity was confined by the shape of the plot, by municipal by-laws and regulations, and by the client's dictates and budget.

'Alright,' he would concede wielding a rubber, 'if you do not want this door then we will simply take it out.'

After such sessions the three of us would go to Panini's on St George's Mall and drink double espressos. As we sipped at the coffee the hard light would dim in his eyes and I'd know that we had survived.

Shortly after these torrid meetings he produced the final plans. We were now so familiar with the layout of the house that it felt as if we'd lived there. We still couldn't fully appreciate the volume of the rooms or even imagine how they would finally feel but we knew what it would be like to lie on our bed gazing at False Bay. The plans were submitted to the municipality and ten days later a building official phoned to say they had been rejected.

'There are nineteen amendments we require,' he said with what I imagined was a tone of triumph.

'Are they major changes?' I replied, trying to suppress my concern. It was late April. The builders I had asked to quote said they needed at least a month to arrive at accurate costings. If the municipality was now asking for major changes the process could be set back by weeks, months even.

'Not really,' said the official. 'Most of them are small technical alterations. But I'm afraid you're going to have to change your roof. You can't have corrugated iron.'

This was hardly a small technical alteration, especially as the roof material had been a major planning concern. Given the pitch of the roof and the open rafters inside, corrugated iron sheeting solved a design detail. It also appealed to my inherent romanticism because corrugated iron has a long tradition as a building material in South Africa. For most Victorian houses corrugated iron sheeting was the quintessential roof covering. More to the point, the mining villages that were erected on the veld with the discovery of diamonds and then gold in the late nineteenth century were made of corrugated iron. The roof was how I wanted to 'reference' – as the jargonists would have it – this history.

Another consideration was that corrugated iron was the cheapest roofing material on the market.

I couldn't guess the municipality's objections to corrugated iron, especially as we would hardly be setting a precedent in the area, and the product was being used on many extremely expensive houses and certainly had no aesthetic detractions.

'Why do we have to change our roof?' I asked.

'The township conditions state that you can only have cement tiles or painted Victorian profile fibre cement sheets,' I was told.

'But what about the other houses with corrugated iron roofs?'

I could sense him shrug at my exasperation.

'This is the township regulation,' he repeated.

The pitch of our roof meant that tiles were out of the question. The painted Victorian profile fibre cement sheets would have had much the same effect as the corrugated iron except they were aesthetically less pleasing. The capping was ugly and because the sheets were small an unsightly line would be created on the slope of the roof. On top of that they faded fast and soon looked shabby. More specifically there was a cost implication: the sheets were heavy so the roof trusses would have to be larger and closer together. The effect inside would be of clutter rather than openness and balance. And then Jill phoned a manufacturer of the fibre cement sheets and learnt that they contained ten percent asbestos fibre.

'Most first world countries have banned the use of asbestos,' she exploded. 'I'm not living in a house with asbestos on the roof.'

She phoned the director of building survey at the municipality and explained the situation to him. They discussed the aesthetics of corrugated iron versus asbestos fibre cement sheets. He admitted that to the layman there was no difference. She pointed out that as every conceivable roofing material was used in Glencairn Heights from thatch, tiles, and slate to wooden shingles and corrugated iron, she couldn't understand why we were being discriminated against. The conversation swung further into the realms of aesthetics, touching not only on materials but styles of architecture. Unsolicited the director told her that every time he drove past Glencairn Heights he averted his eyes so as not to be offended by the hideous architecture. Jill ignored this but wanted to know what were his opinions about asbestos.

'I have recently built a house and I made sure there was no asbestos anywhere,' he said.

'Then why should we have to put up with it.'

The answer, of course, was because of the regulations. The discussion, as always happens when dealing with the municipality, had come full circle. There could be no resolution through an appeal to logic.

Despite our agitation the architect dealt with the amendments as if they were so much technical chaff. Which I suppose they were. He recommended that we accept the municipality's conditions.

'The way it works,' he explained, 'is that you first get the plans approved. Once that's happened we will submit a motivation for a change of plans regarding the roofing material. It's simply a technicality which they're bound to approve. Or you can just go ahead and use the corrugated iron. It's quite likely the building inspector won't even notice when he signs off the house. You've really got to look closely to distinguish between the asbestos sheets and the corrugated iron.'

We decided we'd pursue the legal course once the plans were passed.

11: *Fire And Rain*

At the end of summer and a few weeks into autumn two disasters disturbed the quiet lives in Glencairn Heights.

March is fire month in the mountains around Cape Town. Almost every year the brush burns and this year was no exception. After a long dry summer, one of the driest on record with no rain between January and March, a careless woodchopper's cooking fire set light to Black Hill above Glencairn. The bush was thick, the undergrowth a tinder of dead wood. Fanned by a gusting wind from the south west the fire caught, spread, and roared towards the houses on the slopes of Glencairn mountain.

Between our plot and the bush was an overgrown firebreak. Our neighbours behind us and higher up the road had mere metres between them and the flames. For a day, a night and another day, while firemen with hoses and bulldozers wearily kept at a blaze that showed no signs of lessening, they lived from moment to moment ready to flee. The air became ash. The light was orange. Heat throbbed in the walls of their homes. They feared the worst. Until the wind turned blowing the fire back on itself and people realised they had escaped.

'You cannot believe what it was like,' said our neighbour of the green track suit pants who had been so keen on dissuading us from buying the plot. 'We couldn't open the windows because of the ash and the fire made it too hot for us to sleep. Nobody knew what was going to happen next. And with that noise of the flames it was frightening.'

He was understandably animated by the experience. The fire may have been terrifying, it had also been thrilling, and he and his family had survived unscathed. He praised the firemen, recounted anecdotes of their bravery and endurance, couldn't stop the spew of words that told of his relief. But eventually, as I expected eventually it had to, the conversation came round to our plot, more specifically, our building intentions.

'You know I tried to buy this plot two months ago,' he said. 'I went to the building survey department at the municipality and they told me it was still registered in the previous owner's name so

I phoned the old man and asked to buy it. He told me he'd sold it to you last August. But it's not registered in your name.'

'I can assure you it is,' I replied. 'The transfer went through last September. We've got the deeds.'

'I've tried to buy this land many times,' he went on. 'But before the old man wouldn't sell it and now when I've got the money he tells me it's sold already.' He grimaced at the injustice of this.

I glanced at the estate agent's board not two metres away that bore a large decal reading: 'Sold by us.' The board had been there for seven months. At least twice a day he must've driven past it.

Clearly why he'd been snooping round the building survey department was not to see if the land was still for sale but to find out if we'd submitted plans and if so what impact our house would have on his lower property. I reassured him that our house would be well within the building height restrictions.

'You don't have to worry,' I said. 'There's plenty of space for us to build without getting near the legal limitation.'

'That's good,' he said. 'Because we're all up here for the view.'

The second disaster to afflict Glencairn Heights happened just three weeks later with the start of the autumn rains. Usually these are drenching showers without the gales of winter. But on this proverbially dark and stormy night the downpour was long and excessive and the fire-denuded sands of Black Hill had nothing to bind them. The rain fell. The springs welled up. The dry courses began to flow. And the sand turning to mud, started to slide. This grey soup of ash and sand poured down the natural ditches and sloots and smashed into garden walls that collapsed under the impact as the mud bulldozed on, buckling doors, breaking windows, filling houses. People woke to find it swirling about their beds, a torrent of sludge that had passage through their houses.

Fortunately, once again, our plot was spared. The mud slide crossed our street lower down causing considerable damage to a house below the road but everyone else on the cul-de-sac was voluble with their narrow escape. For a sedate middle-class suburb, Glencairn Heights was suddenly a place of high excitement. Which made it all the more attractive.

When the quotes to build the house started coming in, I was staggered at the cost. The second quote was higher than the first and, for some reason, excluded the wooden deck. Fortunately I'd never intended using either of these builders but needed the quotes to establish what business analysts call a 'benchmark'. The third quote was a detailed document of five pages and, most importantly, was lower than the first two. This builder was and always had been a serious contender. To use an old-fashioned concept, he seemed a gentleman. During the initial briefing he'd listened and explained and offered alternatives and we'd both been impressed. He appeared to be a man we could work with if our first choice and the final quote proved inaccessible. Which it was. Higher than any of the others by at least another quarter, we couldn't give it a moment's serious consideration.

By now we'd become used to the size of the price tag – in fact it was disconcerting how quickly we'd come to accept the large numbers – and were even talking about the quote as a good deal. Of course this good deal didn't include floor tiles, sanitary ware, door handles, lights, a kitchen of any sort, or even the garage door. For these we had a separate budget which some rudimentary trawls through the bathroom boutiques, tile emporiums, and lighting showrooms revealed as hopelessly underestimated. Actually there was no way we could get anywhere near covering these costs.

Nevertheless we signed a contract with the gentleman builder that said he would start the following month, July, and finish on December 17th.

As the plans were passed all that remained to be done was get approval for the corrugated iron roof. We prepared a long letter of motivation that cited the health risk of living with an asbestos product and moved on to a discussion of aesthetics before pointing out that we were hardly setting a precedent as corrugated iron formed the roof of our neighbour's house as well as those of a number of others in the vicinity.

The municipality also required our five immediate neighbours to sign the plans and declare that they had no objections to our choice of roofing material. I could foresee no problems here except that our neighbour of the green track suit pants would probably react adversely when he realised how much of the view his second house was going to lose. If he refused to sign our application would be automatically rejected.

Our plan was to collect his signature last. As we went from one neighbour to the next I could see him watching us from his lounge windows.

We knocked and were invited in. On his dining-room table we laid out the plans. It did not take him long to react.

'But this is a pitched roof,' he exploded. 'How can you have a pitched roof? You can't go higher than my window sills.'

I pointed out to him the contour line on which the house would be built and that as he could see on the diagram we were a metre below the municipality's height restriction.

'No, no. This is impossible. You are going to take away all my view. When I bought that house the building inspectors told me that nobody could build a house higher than my window sills. And now you come with this.'

My neighbour's situation was this: ten years ago he bought a house that had been built on the lowest part of a long steep plot. To exacerbate matters the house site had been levelled according to the lowest contour line and took no advantage of the natural slope. Over the years he tried to buy the plot in front – our plot – because he knew that one day the views from this house would be compromised. But life handed him one of its hard cards when his teenaged son was involved in a car accident and left a quadriplegic. He had to turn his attention to catering for the needs of his son. He decided to sub-divide his plot and build on the upper slope, that way he would retain his views forever and have a house designed to accommodate his son. The lower house could be rented, a handy supplement to his income. Perhaps once he'd recovered financially he would then seek to ensure the views of the lower house by purchasing the erf in front of it.

Most of this worked out, except the last part. And now he was confronting the eventuality he'd dreaded all these years. I knew we were going to take away his lower house's sea views. Given the position of the building we would have needed to build underground to preserve his tenant's view. But we had complied with the building height regulations which had been in force prior to his buying the offended property, and I could see as he grew increasingly excited that he had no idea of the building regulations in the area. This despite having built his new house in the last two years. Yet he did not know that the height of our house was determined by the mean contour level of his full – unsubdivided – plot.

'You can't build like this,' he said. 'There must be some mistake. Have you had these plans passed?'

I nodded.

'This is impossible.'

His voice was raised now, and Jill and his wife who had been talking to one side, turned towards us in consternation.

'Look at this,' he appealed to his wife. 'They're going to take away our view. There's going to be no view from our house any more.'

He meant the lower house, the house he rented out.

We decided to conduct a site inspection. But when we stood on his lower property, the plans held between us, he became even more disturbed about the coming prospect.

'I don't want to tell you what sort of house to build but I didn't think anyone would build a house like this,' he said, his face tight, his lips dry with small flecks of white in the corners of his mouth. 'I always thought whoever built here would build down there.'

'Down there' literally was down there. The plot sloped steeply and to have built on that slope would have provided us with excellent views of our lower neighbour's unattractive wall.

'You do accept that we're allowed to build on our plot,' Jill put in.

'Of course,' he retorted dismissively.

'You must've accepted that at some time someone would build here,' Jill persisted.

'We did try to buy this plot in January,' said his wife. 'We're not lying you know. We did try.'

The four of us stood looking but not seeing the view which would disappear from that vantage point.

'Those people were forced to lower their roof,' he said to his wife pointing at a house across the street. 'They were made to come down a metre.'

96

'I'm sure there must be some way we can compromise,' she suggested. 'We want to settle this amicably.'

I couldn't understand what she meant by a compromise. Certainly she wasn't using the word in any recognisable sense because I failed to see what negotiable options they could offer. Nor did it seem to me that anything needed to be 'settled'.

'Why don't you go to the municipality and satisfy yourselves that we've done everything correctly and that our plans are approved, and then we can talk again,' I suggested, writing our names and telephone number on a piece of paper. 'Please phone us when you've got all the facts.'

We never heard directly from him again. But we did hear that first thing the next morning he was in the offices of the building inspector demanding to know why our plans had been passed. He also challenged our land surveyor's plans because the contour lines didn't conform with those on his diagrams. He was told his contour lines were wrong and it was presumably pointed out to him that our plans were according to regulations. Unconvinced he took the matter to the director of the department, only to be told that the lower echelons knew what they were talking about. Even this was not good enough. He appealed to the ward councillor and she called for the file and told him there was nothing that could be done. Finally, the municipality resorted to the town planner, now retired, who had originally laid out the township, but once more the finding was in our favour.

All this trickled back to us and gave us long nights of worry. What I couldn't understand was why he never phoned to discuss the matter. I puzzled over this. It was what I'd expected but his call never came. I did suspect, however, that the matter wasn't settled. And I anticipated that when construction started he would have the building inspector on site at any real or perceived deviation from the plans.

12: An Aside 2

Towards the end of June, still agitated by our neighbour-to-be and wanting a change of scenery, I drove up to Springbok because the skull of the renegade Koos Sas was much on my mind. I wanted to know more about his death and where he had been shot.

As I turned off the N7 onto the two kilometre approach to Springbok I thought of constables Jurie Dreyer, Karel Esterhuys, and Jan Jurie riding down this road, in those days a dirt track, and into the hills opposite on the hot summer's morning that they hunted down Koos Sas. Not that I spared too much sympathy for Koos Sas, he was a murderer and a thief, a malcontent at odds with society. Had he been born two hundred years earlier his life might have been easier, his death might not have been violent. On the other hand what was the use of such speculation! There was what happened, and what happened was extraordinary.

The story of Koos Sas was not well remembered in Springbok. In the coloured community it was not remembered at all. Among the whites, Jopie Kotze of the Springbok Lodge and Restaurant, remembered some of the details but even he was retelling a story. The generation who were alive on 8 February 1922, the day Jurie Dreyer shot Koos Sas, were no more.

In fact the remaining memory Springbok had of that day was a postcard-size photograph of Koos Sas in the museum. The photograph was encased in a black frame. It stood on a small oak washtable which had been placed next to a brass double bed. Like so many dorp museums this one was also given to a collection of the bric-a-brac of nineteenth century white lives. That the museum was housed in the old synagogue which was closed in 1972 because there were no Jews left in the town said as much about changing times as the collected items themselves. That the synagogue building was given new life when the museum opened in 1991 in honour of the memory of Joseph and Rebecca Jowell, who started the well-known Jowell's Transport back in the thirties, was yet another root into history. Go further along that root and you found Abraham Jowell who came from Lithuania in the 1880s and 'smoused' throughout the Namaqualand region from a mule cart. But that was another story.

On the oak washtable the curator of the Namaqualand Museum had leant the photograph of Koos Sas against a mirror on either side of which were enamel water jugs. Two enamel soap dishes had been arranged in front of the mirror. These domestic items belied the nature of the postcard. The photograph was postcard-size because it actually was a postcard – one that the dominee had had printed.

The inscription at the top of the photograph read in Afrikaans: 'The proceeds of the sale of this card go to the ACVV in Namaqualand.' ACVV stood for the Afrikaanse Christelike Vroue Vereniging. The caption at the bottom read: 'Koos Sas, the murderer of the son of Ds Botha of Stellenbosch in 1917. Three times caught and three times escaped, eventually on 8 February 1922, while attempting to flee, shot dead by policeman Jurie Dreyer on Droodaap [sic], near Springbok, Namaqualand.'

The postcard showed Koos Sas being propped up by Jan Jurie, the first coloured policeman in Springbok. Sas was dressed in an assortment of ragged clothes, his chest exposed. Constable Jurie Dreyer wearing a fedora stood to one side pointing at the dead man.

This photograph – and another that was published in *Die Landstem* on 23 September 1950 – were taken by 12-year-old Willempie Steenkamp, the son of the local dominee W P Steenkamp. They'd gone out to Droëdap either with the constables or after the event to witness the end of Koos Sas. Their exact part in the final moments of Koos Sas was unclear, but then, like all good stories, so much in the life and death of Koos Sas was unclear. What was clear was that the photographs Willempie took were prized by those who participated in the manhunt.

Unlike so many Karoo towns that seem to have collapsed under economic despair and alcoholism, Springbok – and Namaqualand – appeared relatively affluent. People were better dressed, they drove new cars. The streets were active with tourists. Coffee shops had opened, as had a Backpackers, and the Springbok Lodge was now merely one of many bed and breakfast establishments. Outside the town, the garden suburb of Simonsig had all the attributes of big city suburbia without a hint that its origins lay in a forced removal that razed the coloured houses and moved the families over the koppie to what was now Bergsig. Despite this trauma some in Bergsig had prospered, judging by the size of their houses.

Jopie Kotze of the Springbok Lodge was a large affable man with a voice that had been enriched by the tar of a million cigarettes. He knew about the Koos Sas story but he suggested I drove out along the Droëdap road to Peet Markram's place and asked him. 'I had a stroke last year and I can't remember things so well anymore,' he confessed.

At Peet Markram's place I met Lilla Markram who explained her husband was in town for the day. We stood at the chicken-wire fence that surrounded her house and after a short conversation she suddenly closed her eyes and recited one of her poems called 'Swerftog' – literally a wandering journey. This wandering didn't refer to Koos Sas but to the condition of most people living in Namaqualand. Afterwards she directed me to Willie Mostert farther down the road.

'He'll tell you the story,' she said, 'Koos Sas was killed on their land.'

Willie Mostert was seventy-eight years old. On a porch outside the kitchen he lowered himself stiffly on to an old car seat, inviting me to sit opposite on a wooden bench. His blue eyes were rheumy and he was so deaf I had to shout my questions. Although he built the house himself it belonged, in style and content, to the nineteenth century.

Willie Mostert's story about the final moments of Koos Sas differed in many respects from the accepted version. In Willie Mostert's story Koos Sas wasn't buried where he fell because he fell half way up the mountain and it would have taken a man with a jackhammer all day to break out even a shallow grave. No, he was buried down at the farm Droëdap where the doctor – called to conduct a post mortem – cut off the renegade's head and took it away for scientific purposes. There was no mention of the dominee or the dominee's son or the photographs he took. There was no mention of the subsequent exhumation or the boiling of the bones although there was a sick joke that the doctor suggested Koos Sas should be rendered into soap. As far as Willie Mostert was concerned Koos Sas – sans skull – was in his grave on Droëdap although no one knew where that grave was anymore.

Willie Mostert then directed me up the mountain to a kokerboom that had his father's initials carved into it. 'It was near this kokerboom that Koos Sas died,' he said, 'shot through the heart by a single bullet from Jurie Dreyer's Lee Metford.' I found the tree. I sat in its sparse shade gazing at the high mountains either side of this long valley. Nothing moved: the only sound was the low whine of insects. I wondered if this was where Koos Sas really died. Who could say?

When I got back to the farm house Willie Mostert asked, 'Did you see the blood spot?'

I laughed and told him yes. There was not so much as a spark of humour in his eyes or a twitch to his lips. He merely nodded. Then shook my hand and wished me a safe journey home.

13: TB – A City In Trauma

During the month before building started I worked on a second assignment for the *Cape Times'* One City, Many Cultures initiative. This time I was asked to report on the city's health. Once I'd gone through statistics that revealed one of the highest rates of murder, rape, assault, and child abuse in the country, and been told that alcohol was a factor in almost all violent crime and in the alarming number of car accidents that killed and maimed thousands of people each year, a psychological portrait of a deeply disturbed city began to develop. A city in trauma. But if any one factor emerged as a metaphor for this trauma it was a disease that had been a scourge of the city for three centuries – tuberculosis. TB.

According to the statistics, Cape Town had the unhappy distinction of being the TB capital of the world, and it had been for a long time. Why this should be wasn't understood, or even a question worth asking by those, like Mariette Williams, who literally devoted their lives to fighting the disease. She was a young social worker with the TB Care Association, a non-governmental agency that worked closely with the Cape Town city council. Her office was in Manenberg.

In a preliminary phone call she suggested that we meet outside the Philippi police station. She made this arrangement firmly in the tone of voice I suspected she might use with a difficult patient.

I had been trying to make a more complicated set of arrangements because I was worried about my car. Not once had I mentioned this concern but Mariette knew the unease of strangers about the slum of Manenberg. She knew Manenberg existed for many – myself included – like an intimation of the apocalypse, an out-take from the movie *Blade Runner.*

'It's quiet at the moment,' she reassured me, 'your car will be alright.'

We met as stipulated and I followed her the short distance to the Manenberg Clinic. A short distance but far enough to separate one reality from another. It was nine o'clock in the morning but already there were groups of men everywhere: lounging outside backyard gates, standing on the corners, leaning against posts. An old man sitting on an upturned plastic bottle container talked animatedly to a passer-by. There was something timeless in the cameo: a young man listening to an old man's story. The streets were active, noisy with running children and dogs and women, their hair in curlers beneath doeks, watching and smoking. Yet the streets also looked as they appear after a riot: littered with stones and half-bricks and smashed bottles and oddments of clothing.

The clinic was surrounded by a high fence of concrete poles and an automatic gate. The street was visible between the poles but gangsters couldn't run in during their wars and use the clinic as part of the battleground, which happened before the fence was erected. During the worst of the gang wars in 1998 the clinic was forced to shut for three months but reopened in small offices on the other side of Manenberg. These were inconvenient and cramped but this was an emergency and at least the clinic was up and running. 'We were proud of that,' said Mariette. 'Let's just hope it doesn't happen again.'

We went inside and she found a small backroom where we could talk. Somewhere in the clinic a baby whined unceasingly.

Mariette was a University of Cape Town graduate. She was born and raised in the city. She was committed to her work and she talked honestly and bluntly about it and the conditions under which she had to work. She said if she told me her salary, I'd laugh. She admitted to occasionally being resentful that it was so low but then she chuckled and said: 'That's NGO work, that's the reality.' The thing was she couldn't imagine being or doing anything else. For Mariette this was an exciting, relevant job. To use a war metaphor: a matter of being in the front line of what she called the 'TB-HIV onslaught.'

With an incidence of five hundred and sixty people per hundred thousand, TB thrived among the poverty-stricken where living conditions were overcrowded and people's diet was haphazard and the stress of unemployment, lack of money, and alcoholism ground into the daily life. On a map of Cape Town great parts of the city would be shaded by these conditions. Also TB was what Mariette and her colleagues called an 'opportunistic disease' – an airborne bacteria ready to hook into the lungs of anyone whose immune system might be ailing. Anyone, say, who was HIV positive. A statistic had it that forty percent of those with HIV could develop TB.

This was of great concern to the people monitoring the city's health. They spoke of TB now manifesting itself in the white population where it had been virtually unknown for decades. They talked, as Mariette did, of an onslaught.

'Consider,' said Mariette, 'as you walk down St George's Mall, forty percent of the people you pass probably will have been infected with TB.'

Which was why TB had been declared a health emergency in the city and a treatment strategy developed by the World Health Organisation instituted in an attempt to contain the risk. The nature of TB was such that it required six months of dedicated treatment. Six months of daily medication. If the medication was stopped after a few weeks or months the complications that set in were alarming, both for the patient and for society. Within a few months they would become ill again but by now the TB bacillus would have mutated and the original medicine was no longer effective. The cost of treating a patient with drug resistant TB was R35 000, against a cost of R3 500 for the 'ordinary' version of the disease. And patients who were drug resistant transmitted a TB strain that was drug resistant, in other words, a strain that was expensive and difficult to cure.

'There are just two simple statistics we have to remember,' said Mariette. 'The first is that eighty percent of TB patients only go to a clinic long after they've contracted the disease. The second is that one person can infect twenty others through contact in the street, train, taxi, and café.'

A top priority for Mariette was to make sure people took their medicine. This was where the WHO programme was having some success. Under this strategy volunteers from a particular community became 'care supporters' and saw to it that TB patients took their pills daily. After a five-day training workshop the supporters took over the function that would normally be the responsibility of a nurse at a clinic. But because there weren't enough nurses, let alone enough clinics, having 'care supporters' in the immediate community meant there was a greater chance of sufferers staying the course.

In Manenberg there were one hundred and forty patients and twenty care supporters with a maximum of ten clients each. It was part of Mariette's job to supply the back-up to these care supporters. Which was no easy task at the best of times, and nothing short of impossible during the periodic gang wars.

'I'm not a fearful person,' she told me, 'but about a year ago while I was sitting in this very office I heard shooting. These were serious guns and that was the first time I felt scared. Nowadays I phone ahead to find out what's happening here. And when I'm here, I'm careful. I watch what's going on in the street, I drive with the windows up, I keep the doors locked, that sort of thing. When it's quiet or there are flashy cars driving around you know there's going to be trouble.

'I'll tell you one thing, the care supporters helped us enormously through the gang wars. Even under those desperate conditions we had a really good compliance rate. People would wait until the shooting died down then duck out and run to the care supporters. I think it's because a strong relationship develops between the patient and the care supporter who lives here, who knows what's going on, so that even during the worst times people will do their utmost to get their medicine. The only thing that sometimes concerns me is that if I get shot there has to be some contingency plan. And I don't mean get shot in that I'm being targeted, but that I get caught in the crossfire.'

Mariette said this as if she'd said nothing particularly out of the ordinary. How many people, I wondered, had that consideration at the back of their minds as they went about their daily jobs? It was a measure of her personality that she quickly added: 'Can you imagine what it's like to live here under these conditions?'

We left the clinic and drove to a care supporter called Anne, who lived in a quiet side street where the fences on either side were of corrugated iron. Anne supported seven patients. She was short and open-faced with a ready smile but also, I suspected, a will of iron. Each week she went to the clinic to fetch the medicine for her patients and every day they came to her home to receive their tablets. For this Anne received a token gratuity of R40 a patient. 'The money helps,' she laughed, 'of course, yes, but I'm not doing this for the money. I'm doing this because I want to help people.'

One of her patients was Isah, thirty-eight years old and unemployed. He'd been diagnosed with TB shortly after losing his job.

'My dream is to be healthy again,' he said. 'I want to get a job when the treatment's finished so that I can support my family. In the end it's up to you to look after your own life, not so!'

Mariette took the long way back to the clinic. We passed a row of burnt-out shops where the owners refused to pay protection money to the gangs and were closed down and then looted. We passed huge graffiti that was dark and evil and the one featured the gangster icon, Tupac Shakur. We passed a dog in a gutter that Mariette said had been lying there for two days. It was still twitching.

'There is a malaise here,' said Mariette. 'As if this whole community is suffering from depression. I've worked in Guguletu and it's not like this.' She was frustrated, desperately wanting things to change but not knowing how to go about it.

I remembered Isah's words: 'Manenberg is mos, well, Manenberg. You get robbed with a knife at your throat just getting bread. It's disgusting. It's not the way to live.'

A week later I joined another TB Care social worker at a factory. Ursula Poggenpoel was a no-nonsense woman with a sound grasp of the Cape Flats vernacular. For thirty minutes she had a bunch of workers listening closely to her even though it was lunch time and they'd been working all morning and would much rather have been eating their lunch and joking among themselves.

She picked on the smokers first and soon no one was smoking any more. Not that she'd criticised them, merely told them one or two things about the state of their lungs. Then she ran through the TB symptoms: coughing, tiredness, hot flushes, irritability, weight loss, spitting up blood. She started talking about alcoholism: what she called Friday night alcoholism, weekend alcoholism, or day on day alcoholism.

She mentioned the quantities of liquor bought for weekend parties. Astounding quantities. She mentioned shebeens like Jesus and Hoender where supplies could be acquired once Friday's stocks had run out. She talked about fishermen who went away for the weekend with more booze than food. Some of the men squirmed with embarrassment. They nudged one another like little boys caught out. They knew she'd got their number.

Ursula broke into Flats Afrikaans. She described wasted weekends. Weekends not only of drink but of dagga and mandrax, and anything that could be smoked. She talked about drunk and drugged men falling on their faces, 'earthing,' after they'd smoked dagga, and some of the workers slapped their thighs and wiped their hands over their faces, bashful, almost guilty that they'd been exposed. And in their own language.

Yet Ursula didn't criticise, merely stated matters bluntly. She talked about TB and its treatment bluntly too. I'd had it described to me five times in the last few days but listening to Ursula was like hearing it for the first time and it wasn't nice. I looked at the faces of the men: they were concentrating, listening to her.

After the session we talked for a while before she left and she told of her maternal grandfather who was so colonial English he insisted on high tea with cucumber sandwiches and of her paternal grandfather who was Boer Afrikaans. 'My family's all so wonderfully mixed up,' she laughed, 'so mixed. Actually, you could say I grew up white' – and she used the term as a synonym for middle class. 'Home, church, school, family, a very closed circle. I was eighteen before I found out about the Cape Flats'.

While doing her nursing training at Victoria Hospital in Wynberg she got to see another side of life that was about drink and dagga. 'I saw my friends doing that too. It was sad. Awful.' Then her face cleared. 'But I wouldn't change this job for anything. It's an absolute challenge. I really enjoy it.' A pause. 'Although there are some days when it's difficult getting out of bed. But then we all feel like that, don't we?' She chuckled.

And with that Ursula who loved classical music and pasta and walking in Kirstenbosch Gardens drove off.

The next day I visited a clinic in Hout Bay. There were a few young women with their babies in the waiting room when I arrived. They were early, so was I. The mothers put the children on the floor in a group and fetched them toys from a box. The pre-toddlers played happily and their mothers talked about family matters.

Every now and then old men came in and went through the waiting room to a door in a passageway marked with the initials TB. A few moments later they sauntered out and headed off into the day. Then a women entered the clinic with a baby strapped to her back. She ignored the other mothers, heading for the TB room.

Eventually I heard the baby crying, not a howl but a low insistent anguish. It went on and on.

In the room with the mother and baby was Christine Ndude. She'd been at the clinic since it opened an hour earlier to make breakfast for the TB patients who came daily to receive their medicine. Christine was a voluntary worker, paid a small gratuity by the TB Care Association. She was also a sangoma. She was doing this work because she wanted to help and she wanted to heal the sick.

Right now she was having difficulty in getting the baby to swallow the medicine. She ended up squirting it down the child's throat with a syringe. Both mother and child were HIV positive. The baby had TB.

'We're seeing more and more of this,' commented Nomfundo Memani, a social worker from the TB Care Association, as we stood in the doorway, looking on. 'It's a big problem.'

Once the mother and baby were treated we sat in a backroom and Christine told her story in Xhosa. Nomfundo translated. What unfolded was complex and compelling.

One of Christine's parents had been a sangoma and, according to tradition, she inherited the 'sickness'. This first manifested itself in aberrant behaviour when she was twelve years old. She started skipping school, was disobedient to her parents, spent hours with the initiates in the bush. Once she disappeared for a number of days and was found smeared with white mud in a river. She was clutching beads which she said the ancestors of the river had given her, and carried a bucket that sangomas use. For a few days she vomited badly. Only then did people recognise her calling. At home a sheep was slaughtered to give thanks to the ancestors. She was sent to receive instruction from other sangomas but she found it unhelpful because the sort of medicine her patients needed was presented to her in dreams.

'It is a gift from God,' she said.

And did it not conflict with Western medicine?

'No,' she replied. The TB medicine worked. She could not cure TB sufferers with herbs. But she could use traditional medicines for other uses.

The talk moved to the power of the ancestors. 'If the ancestors call, you have to go,' said Nomfundo. 'It doesn't matter if you are in a board meeting, or it is three o'clock in the morning. You have to go immediately.'

She said she was always aware of the ancestors. She should sacrifice an animal to them to give thanks for her successes. But, she laughed, 'I'm too stingy.' Nomfundo's successes were singular. While working as a part-time packer at a Pick 'n Pay supermarket she attended the University of the Western Cape and graduated in social sciences. Pick 'n Pay gave her a bursary for three of her four years of study.

'It's important to make a sacrifice to the ancestors,' she said, 'otherwise they may no longer bless my life.'

For a moment I could see the tensions in Nomfundo's life. She stared at me and I couldn't hold her gaze. Then she relented and looked out the window at the far sand dunes.

'You know,' she said, 'there are some educated, wealthy black people who die of TB. They are too embarrassed to go to the clinic. They think TB is a sign of poverty. They go to a private doctor and they get the medicine but they only take it until they feel better. Then they get sick again and maybe this time they are drug resistant and they die.

'This stigma is terrible. It is like that with HIV, too.'

14: *Building On Virgin Sand*

On Friday morning 9 July 1999 we met the builder on site to ratify the proposed levels, boundaries and pegs. The moment was as profound as it was meant to be. The morning clear, dewed, threads of cobweb glistening between the bushes: the start of the future. About us people left for work or took their children to school. Some waved, some smiled, all exuding an apparent goodwill. Except that in his eyrie above us, paced our disgruntled neighbour monitoring our unwelcome activity.

The previous afternoon, using stakes and twine, the builders had laid out the shape of the house and we could now – pushing aside fynbos, stepping round rocks, leaping a hole, sinking into the sand – walk through the 'rooms'. As we went I carefully monitored the view. Which was when, with a feeling of anxiety bubbling in my stomach, I realised that the house in front of us was small. Seriously small. If it were sold the new owners might extend along to the right and that glorious sight of sand and sea and sky could be reduced to a holiday postcard. Become merely a cherished memory.

What the neighbour's agitation at our plans had done was to increase our awareness of the potential problems and here was one right in front of us that I hadn't noticed before. Despite all the careful deliberations before we bought the plot neither of us had paid any attention to the size of the house in front. Should we stop right now, I thought. At this stage we're only in for the price of the plot. But it was too late, the dice had been cast way back in Berlin. Perhaps there was an alternative.

'Can we slide the house further along the site?' I asked the builder.

'Oh yes,' he replied, 'it's commonly done. You simply submit rider plans at the end of the contract.'

I breathed out quietly.

So the house was slipped along two metres and in the process dropped to a contour a metre below our designated building platform.

'That should please the neighbour,' said Jill. 'Now we're two metres under the height restriction.'

As it turned out he wasn't at all pleased. The moment we left to recover our equilibrium at the Olympia Deli over cappuccinos and croissants the neighbour phoned the building inspector, demanding his immediate presence on site.

Over the next week Jill and I only visited the site twice. Each time the foundations were deeper and the builders seemed to have every intention of digging on.

'How deep do you have to go?' I asked peering into the trenches, concerned that while the cuttings went down the contract price for bricks was going to be readjusted into dizzy realms.

'Until we reach virgin sand,' replied the builder.

Virgin sand baffled me both as a concept and a reality. Virgin ground I could understand: it had a tactile, unbroken presence, the connotations of being untouched by human hands. But sand was different. Sand was so much more obviously separate grains. Given the individuality of sand what determined the reality of a cohesive virgin community? The answer to this grave metaphysical question was a stick. Any old stick.

'What you do,' explained the builder, 'is push the stick into the sand. As soon as you start meeting resistance you're up against virgin territory.'

As an adolescent I'd read books with titles like 'Growing into Manhood' which phrased sex in much the same way.

'As simple as that?'

'As simple as that,' he confirmed, although I could tell he felt diminished by having to disclose such an intricate part of the inner mystic of building science.

I tried my hand with the stick. Virgin sand seemed to be as remote as once had been the hilly country described in 'Growing into Manhood.'

A week later the builder called us to a site meeting with the

110

architect and the structural engineer. I soon understood that the purpose of the meeting was to explain to us how much more money we'd have to spend to secure the foundations.

Our problems were twofold: at the spot where our entrance would be was a hole filled with builder's rubbish – broken bricks, plastic, ceiling board, pieces of guttering – presumably dumped there when the neighbour's face-brick house was built. The stick was penetrating through this but not reaching virgin sand. If we didn't want to have our entrance hall sink into unfathomed depths, the structural engineer advised that more steel should be put into the slab. Which seemed a simple solution.

Problem number two was of a greater order. It concerned the study where the search for virgin sand had entailed a large 'cut-back' into the dune that was the essence of our plot. Eventually excavations had bottomed-out on a clay bed and here was a constant pool of water.

'It would seem to be a seep,' proclaimed the builder.

We stood gazing at the yellowy water.

'We're not sure where it's coming from,' added the construction supervisor.

'It never dries up,' mused the builder.

'But then it doesn't get any bigger after rain,' said the supervisor.

I looked at the malevolent pool of water, clearly I was being told this was a big problem. We stood, thoughtful and silent.

'And so?' I queried.

'Well ...' began the builder, 'we've got to do something about it. What we propose is an agricultural drain that goes all the way down the seaward side of the house, cuts across here behind the retaining wall, then proceeds out and away into what may one day be your garden,' he said vaguely indicating the fynbos wilderness that started on the other side of the foundations. 'We've done it before. There's a ninety-nine percent chance of it working but you can never be sure.'

The architect and the structural engineer rubbed their chins.

'Look at it this way,' put in the builder, 'if we hadn't had to dig such deep foundations we'd never have known it was there in the first place.'

This wasn't a totally helpful way of approaching the problem. 'What is the alternative?' I asked.

'That we reposition the house,' said the builder.

Somehow repositioning what already more resembled the bombed remains of a Berlin apartment during World War Two than a house under construction didn't appear to be an option.

Every Saturday in August Jill and I went to the site to gaze in rapture at the progress. By the first weekend the footings were completed, a week later the study walls were up and part of the garage had been built. Then the concrete deck was laid over the study and the slab thrown for the remainder of the house.

Shortly after the concrete deck over the study was installed the neighbour brought a mid-morning halt to the building process when he noticed that our bedroom floor was three steps up from the sitting room floor. He phoned the building inspector. But, as it turned out, everything was the way it should be. Our architect had designed a larger volume for the living area than in other rooms without affecting the roof line. The neighbour, mollified, went home. The building inspector returned to his office. The builders stubbed out their cigarettes. All this I heard second hand. The neighbour was not talking to us, not even to complain.

Not long afterwards I was phoned by the editor of the local community newspaper. She told me she was writing a story on how our house would take away the neighbour's view. She asked me if I was a novelist. I hesitantly said yes, and could almost hear the headlines jangling in her head. Arrogant Writer Blocks Neighbour's View. Do you know your neighbour's situation? she asked. I confirmed that I knew about his paraplegic son. Did I know that he relied on income from his rented house to support his son? I said I couldn't see the relevance of this. She responded that estate agents had calculated that by stealing the view I had devalued his house by some R200 000 – possibly a third of its potential price. I replied that this was speculation as only a sale could determine the price of a property. Nevertheless, she countered, I was now jeopardising the rental income the family derived from that property. There didn't seem to be much point in arguing with a reporter who already appeared to have the story planned so I said I didn't want to deal with this matter through her newspaper. She said I had no choice she was writing the story and what was my comment. No comment, I replied.

This discussion left me uneasy and annoyed but I had been a journalist long enough to know that sometimes there was no changing a reporter's angle and that in those circumstances the least said the better. 'No comment' would sound blunt when weighed against our neighbour's unhappy circumstances, but like everything it would blow over. I couldn't see any other option but to sit out whatever opprobrium would be thrown at us.

And then coincidence placed the reporter and me at the same lunch table the next day. Unexpectedly, I was invited to lunch at a wine estate, and there she was.

'I don't believe this,' she said as we were introduced. 'This is awful.'

I shrugged nonchalantly although inside I praised the universe for its exquisite sense of order. Of course the topic of conversation at the table eventually drifted round to my troublesome house. I got an opportunity to explain about the height restrictions, the placement of the neighbour's house, my one and only meeting with him, and the important detail that he wasn't losing his – or his son's – view. When the devaluation of his house came up the table broke into hoots of laughter at the futility of believing anything estate agents said. 'They'll tell you just what you want to hear,' everyone chorused.

When I stood up to leave the reporter said, 'Won't you consider changing your comment. It doesn't look good for you. You don't want to live in a street where all your neighbours hate you. If you want to make a statement the deadline is 10 o'clock Monday.'

I thought that after all she'd heard she would realise there was no story, but then community newspapers are not known for their acuity. Nor was I concerned about what the neighbours thought.

'No,' I smiled. 'This is just one of those unfortunate things.' I paused: 'But tell me, what does he want out of all this?'

'He wants you to lower your roof,' she replied.

'He's never asked me to,' I responded, baffled.

'If you don't he's going to build a huge wall behind your house that will take away your views down the valley and cut off your sunlight,' she continued.

I could only shake my head in wonderment.

Over the weekend I changed my mind and prepared a statement. On Monday morning I took it to the newspaper's offices and the reporter tacked it to the end of a story which I suspected she'd written before she'd even phoned me. Three days later I opened the newspaper to find a photograph of the neighbour leaning mournfully against his new fence with our walls rising behind him. Next to this was another photograph of the unsullied view before building began. The headline read: 'Neighbours spar over lost sea view.' Not entirely accurate as I wasn't doing any fighting at all.

The report continued with a comment from the director of building survey for the municipality, Bill Carter, who had undertaken an inspection of the offending building and agreed that it was a sad situation. This was the same man who had been against asbestos and thought that the architecture of Glencairn Heights was appalling.

'There is no doubt there is going to be a major effect on their view,' he said. 'There used to be a preservation of view guideline enforced by the Simon's Town municipality [that originally controlled this area] but this could only be applied until it was challenged in law. Now there is big money coming into Simon's Town, and people are increasingly prepared to challenge this sort of guideline.'

My statement summarising the situation from my point of view followed. And that was that. No outraged letters to the newspaper ensued in the following weeks. We had some puzzled enquiries from friends, otherwise nothing. I was annoyed because the neighbour had made no effort to contact us. On the other hand I rather enjoyed Bill Carter's insinuation that I was 'big money' ready to challenge the law at the mere mention of a regulation. The fact that we'd conformed to his department's regulations seemed to be beside the point.

15: The Last Harpooner Of False Bay

One Saturday morning shortly after the publication of the newspaper article I went to the house simply to wander around the 'rooms'.

While I stood in what would be our bedroom gazing at the sea a whale suddenly broke the surface in a huge black arc. Again and again the whale leapt while I stood at the glassless window overcome with the realisation that I was watching this mating ritual from my soon-to-be home. It seemed too dangerous a thought to believe it would come true. I felt I was tempting fate. Playing too obvious a hand in my own life. The whales were one of the reasons we wanted a view of the bay but was this not asking for too much? As the whale leapt again I decided it was and it wasn't. Whales were part of the bay, part of its history. You got one, you got the other.

Some years earlier, in 1996, I had traced the last man on the bay to be trained as a harpooner. He was eighty-seven years old and confined to a wheelchair. There was nothing in his face that belied his career or years: the only grey in his black hair was at his temples and in his sideburns, nor could I describe his features as rugged or lined despite a lifetime spent fishing from ocean-going boats off the western coastline of South Africa and Namibia. He had a quiet voice, so quiet that sometimes it registered as merely a sibilance on the tape recording. He smiled as he told his memories. He told them so fluently that I wondered if he lived more in the past than the present.

The man's name was Cyril Fernandez. We talked in a dim, ground floor Sea Point flat that was rented by his granddaughter and her husband. The sea was at the end of the street but he had no view of it from his room. The only indications of his fishing life were a cast of a giant marlin's head on a chair in a corner and a print of a sailing ship running before the wind hanging on the wall.

In the middle of the nineteenth century his grandfather, Pedro E'ustaquio, a Filipino from Iloilo on the island of Panay, had been shanghaied to help crew a Spanish merchantman and had jumped ship in Simon's Town Bay. At the dead of night – what other time was there! – Pedro swam ashore and walked along the wagon track to Kalk Bay, a fishing village with a reputation as a Filipino haven. There he was taken by the young men to hide in the caves above the village. Of course the Spanish captain came looking for him: cursed the villagers for their deception and offered a ransom for the runaway's return. But the people of Kalk Bay wouldn't give up their secret. In disgust the captain went back to his ship, sailing out the following day.

From his refuge in the mountain E'ustaquio watched the sails of the ship until they disappeared. He was sad: he would never see the Philippines again. But if sadness was the price of freedom, then a new life was worth it. He left his old surname on the mountain. When he walked into Kalk Bay he said, My name's Fernandez. Pedro Fernandez.

There were no dates to this history: it floated in the memory of Cyril Fernandez with all the immediacy of an anthology of short stories. Which was how he told me the story of his parents' marriage:

When the southeaster started blowing a few days before his wedding, Pedro Fernandez (the son of the runaway) got the itch of money in his fingers. But the wind also brought the stench of whale oil to his nostrils so he knew the cash would not come easily. He shrugged, that was the least of his worries, of more importance was to take his beloved to get the blessing of his dying mother. This was a task that filled his heart with dread. As he cleaned fish on the Kalk Bay beach he wondered how he could prove to his mother that the beautiful Lydia Luyt was his.

Lydia was a Claremont girl, a servant of Mr Green the wine merchant, who every summer brought his family to holiday in their cottage near the fishing village. And it was known that young women from the merchants' houses had no eyes for fishermen. So Lydia was a catch way beyond the wildest dreams of Pedro Fernandez. There wasn't a fisherman in Kalk Bay who hadn't tried his charm on her and been spurned. Lydia with her English blood and her soft hands wasn't for them. Pedro knew his mother would be sceptical of this good fortune. Words were not proof enough for her.

When Pedro had finished cleaning the fish he took them to sell to Mr Green. As he approached the cottage he could see Lydia's checked petticoat hanging on the washing line. The sight of it lifting so gently in the breeze mesmerised him. How beautiful it was, how fine between his fingers. Then quickly, unseen, he snipped off a square at the hem and slipped it into his pocket.

The next afternoon Pedro and Lydia took the Cape cart from Kalk Bay to St James where his mother and father had a cottage. Pedro was nervous. He could hardly talk and his Adam's apple juggled in his throat with agitation.

How do I know she's really going to be your wife? the frail Ma-Fernandez breathed at her son.

Just ask to look at her petticoat, he replied.

To Lydia's embarrassment she had to reveal the hem of her petticoat with its missing square.

What does this prove? Pedro's mother demanded in a scratchy voice.

Would I cut this from a stranger's petticoat! declared Pedro flourishing the missing square. Of course not, I would only take it from the woman who was to be my wife.

By the time they got back to Kalk Bay, radiant with the blessings of the old woman on her death bed, the southeaster was set and roaring. Pedro Fernandez looked at the impossible sea and knew there would be good catches when the wind went down. He knew too that with this wind the butcher, grocer, and baker would give him meat, cheese, eggs, bread, vegetables, fruit, dates, nuts, wine, whatever he wanted for the wedding feast. The southeaster guaranteed repayment. In that howling summer gale Pedro and Lydia were married. The wind gave them a week's honeymoon – for no one could put to sea in such a maelstrom – but when one night it stopped, abruptly, unexpectedly, Pedro woke at the sudden quiet. In the early light he and Lydia went down to the beach: washed up on the rocks was a dead whale.

It's ours, he whispered to her. Quick give me your petticoat. We claim the whale.

Poor Lydia, the Claremont girl, awkwardly stepped out of her petticoat and watched as her Pedro tied the garment to an oar and plunged the oar into the whale's blubber.

There, he said, now it's ours.

And then poor Lydia who'd never had to clean a fish watched her husband cut a door into the carcass and disappear into the belly of the beast. Poor Lydia shut her eyes and prayed to the Virgin Mary. When she looked again Pedro stood before her grinning. He was covered in blood and gore. Poor Lydia wanted to faint.

Fetch tins, he told her. Fetch wood and coal.

Under the huge iron cauldrons that Norwegian whalers had long ago abandoned on the beach Pedro built fires.

But why are we doing this? asked Lydia.

You'll see, he replied. And showed her what to do.

For two days Pedro laboured in the slime and ooze and stench and dimness. He cut off strips of fat from the stomach and took them like sacred offerings to his wife. In the cauldrons she melted them down until a fine oil bubbled on the surface which she ladled into the tins.

For two days Pedro and Lydia stank of whale. Their clothes were saturated. Whatever they touched became greasy and contaminated. Lydia wondered if she would smell like this for the rest of her life. It made her want to cry. Don't worry, said Pedro. It'll be worth it.

For those two days the people of Kalk Bay joked about the foolishness of Pedro and Lydia who were so deluded by love as to think they could compete with the Norwegian whalers stationed at Hangklip across the bay. No, it was rank foolishness, the Norwegians had long cornered the market. All these two were doing was smelling the place out with the reek of boiling fat.

Pedro paid no heed. When the job was done, he made a fire in their backyard and destroyed their clothes. No soap on earth could wash the smell and the oil out of them he told Lydia. Clothes were precious she reminded him, thinking longingly of her ruined petticoat. Don't worry, he said to her, soon there would be enough money to buy new trousers and dresses. The best there were.

That night Pedro decanted the oil into old bottles he'd scrounged from the villagers. He cut plugs of wood as stoppers. The next day Pedro took a sack full of bottles to town. He caught the Cape cart to Wynberg and the train to Cape Town. The merchants snapped up his oil. But don't bring us any more, they cautioned him, we're now overstocked.

Pedro went home with money-filled pockets jingling and a new checked petticoat wrapped in tissue paper. He had married the most beautiful girl on the peninsula and she'd turned out to be lady luck. Pedro's heart was singing. He and Lydia would be the envy of Kalk Bay.

And then the southeaster began to blow again. For a week it whipped the bay: the waves seethed against the rocks, dead gannets washed up in the tideline, a salty haze drifted across the mountain. The fishermen talked of steenbras, hottentot, yellowtail, mackerel. Maybe even tunny blown in. Or another whale torn lose from the Norwegian whaling ships. Imagine that, they said. Those Norwegians were always losing whales, perhaps they'd lose another.

Which is what happened. On the morning the wind went down a whale carcass lay on the beach. This time everybody wanted a piece of the prize except Pedro and Lydia. Pedro said he would rather go fishing. Lydia said she had housework to do. You're too late Pedro tried to tell them. You shouldn't compete with the Norwegians. But no one believed him until the merchants of Cape Town, crossing their arms, shaking their heads, said, no, no, no, we don't want any more oil.

Cyril Fernandez recounted the story in his quiet smiling voice. 'My father was a good harpooner,' he added. 'He taught me to be a harpooner, but I never harpooned a whale.'

Cyril Fernandez was born too late. By the time he was old enough to stand in the bow of an open boat being rowed achingly towards a slow-moving southern right, there were few whales coming to mate or calve in False Bay. For one thing their numbers were declining. For another the Norwegians in their steam-powered whaling ships mounted with harpoon guns got them first.

But when Cyril Fernandez was young there were still men on the coast who had the gear and the will to hunt any whale should the opportunity arise. One of these was George Cotton from Tristan da Cunha who had a trekking licence to fish off Simon's Town beach.

Cyril Fernandez: 'There was a man called George Cotton, tall man, darkish. And then there was a whale in the bay. Cotton was trekking on the beach in Simon's Town, Long Beach in Simon's Town, when he got a report that there was a whale in the bay so he went out with his trek boat. He had his gear, his whaling gear, ropes and harpoons and so on.

'At Kalk Bay there was also an old man who had whaling gear, an old coloured Portuguese, Mr Michaels. He came from Cape Verde. He had harpoons and bombs. The old man could get these bombs from Portugal or somewhere. Anyhow. Cotton went out and they harpooned the whale. Now these ropes of his had been lying there in the sheds for so long that naturally they had got dry and rotten and so on. So Cotton's rope broke.

'You know when you harpoon a whale by hand from an open boat it sets off and you play it until it bleeds itself to its death and then you tow it back to shore. There's another story I can tell you about a whale that took the run after it was harpooned and the whale took the run and it ran so far out of False Bay that the crew had to cut the rope and row back home.

'But now Cotton's rope broke and Cotton lost the whale. He did not have bombs so he couldn't kill the whale before it broke his ropes.

'My brother with the skipper of the boat, The Chrissie, saw what had happened and they saw that the whale was coming towards Kalk Bay. So they got a crew together and they rowed out with old Mr Michaels as the harpooner. They got near the whale and they harpooned it. The old man was already so old but he had the true style of the whale harpooner. When they got the whale alongside he jumped on to the whale and drove the lance into the soft spot of the whale and killed it. Then they towed the whale in.

'At that time the harbour was built already. I was a youngster and I was there to watch them bring the whale in. Now Cotton was watching through his binoculars from Simon's Town and he could see the whale had been caught by somebody else. He knows his harpoon is in that whale and as such it means that that whale is his. Cotton came to Kalk Bay on the train and he came onto the long pier. Now he was a tall thin man and had a very gruff voice. When he got in amongst the people looking at the whale he stood on the edge of the harbour there and shouted down to the men in The Chrissie: "I CLAIM THE WHALE!"

'Those few words took them to court. And only then did Cotton realise that the whale did not belong to him even though his harpoon was in it. If his harpoon had had his name, George Cotton, and address then the whale would have been his. But his harpoon was unsigned so he lost the whale.

'The people on The Chrissie didn't have their harpoons signed but they had their ropes attached to it. So Cotton did not have the whale, just a loose harpoon in the whale.'

In *Moby Dick* when Stubb kills a whale Herman Melville writes: '[The whale] rolled not in brine but in blood, which bubbled and seethed for furlongs behind in their wake. The slanting sun playing upon this crimson pond in the sea, sent back its reflection into every face, so that they all glowed to each other like red men.'

Cyril Fernandez: 'You see the dying part takes a long time. The dying part can take a very long time. The harpoon is merely to keep the whale hooked and you wait until it weakens. But the whale can set off with boat and all and later on you are so far away from land that they would rather cut the rope than be drawn right away to sea.

'How quickly the whale dies when it's weakened and alongside all depends on how brave the harpooners are. Usually when the whale is alongside they jump on to the whale to kill it with the lance. They put it in the soft spot.

'They also used bombs. A bomb is about this long [he indicated about sixty centimetres] and about as thick as this [he made a circle with his forefinger and thumb]. You push that bomb into the whale and there is a trigger on the bomb that as it goes into the whale it goes off and the bomb bursts inside the whale. When it bursts it shoots out all little assegais and they break up the whale's blood vessels and what-have-you and the whale dies.'

Cyril Fernandez cleared his throat. He looked at me.

'Those were the ways they killed a whale in the olden times,' he said.

Down below me, off Glencairn beach, the whale was drifting slowly towards Simon's Town. Many decades ago the sight of a whale this close to the shore would have had the harpooner George Cotton launching his boats.

16: Choosing A Toilet

For some incomprehensible reason I have never paid much attention to the aesthetics of toilets (bar the one in Berlin), or, for that matter, the design of basins, taps, shower heads, door handles, or light fittings. They're the kind of items I've always taken for granted, unless they were particularly hideous. Door handles were, well, door handles. Taps were taps. You turned them on, they brought forth water. Toilets were toilets: a bowl and a cistern and there wasn't too much you could do about it.

Or so I thought until the day came to start choosing the sanitary ware, door furniture (as the handles and escutcheons were called), lights et al. Jill seemed to know where to find these things and we ended up in parts of town I didn't know existed, nor do I wish ever to visit those quarters again. But for the record, in the backstreets of remote industrial complexes are a collection of bathroom boutiques, lighting emporia, lock shops, and ceramic tile and slate merchants committed to the middle-class condition. As I wandered, dazed and confused, through opulent overabundance not seen since the prosperity of Berlin, I came to realise that these items defined my life. Those who came to visit us in our new house would pee in our loos and merely from the shape of the toilet make assumptions about whether we were anti the death penalty, had read Walter Mosley, listened to the strident rhythms of the Afro Celt Sound System.

It took three months to decide on the house's accessories. Three months of making decisions and revisions that a minute would invariably reverse. Although we picked the toilets we couldn't decide on the toilet seats. Although we had taps for the basins we couldn't pinpoint a mixer tap for the showers. In the end we chose items from five different bathroom shops – an attention to detail which made our friends smile at us benignly as people condescend to the mad. Even shop assistants looked at us strangely.

When the shower arm was out of stock in one store the salesman's suggestion was: 'Choose another.'

I looked round his showroom at some thirty shower arms on display. Here were various styles imported from Italy, the Scandinavian countries, Australia, the United Kingdom, let alone a plethora of local designs. Didn't he get the point? Didn't he understand that we had chosen this one shower arm over all the others? Of course he didn't know that it had taken us five visits to his showroom – a return trip of close on a hundred kilometres – to arrive at this choice. Nevertheless, as if such decisions could be made on the turn, he smiled at me and said, 'It's only a shower arm.'

'Perhaps,' I suggested, 'you could order one.' How could I begin to explain to him about the elegance of the lines?

He looked crestfallen. 'It's got to be shipped from Italy,' he replied. 'It will take at least three weeks.'

'That's alright,' I said, 'we can wait.'

As we had to wait for the kitchen tap, for the sink, for up-lighters, downlighters, spotlights, and door handles that I was particularly keen on because they resembled stylised versions of the wings at Hermes's feet. Waiting for shipments emphasised how far away we were from the rest of the world. We were, as Cape Town had always been, at the end of the high seas, maybe no longer reliant on trade winds, but certainly reliant on chandlers and international shipping, and the container ships that plied the routes round the Cape opened up by the Portuguese, the Dutch, and the English so long ago.

And then there were items that had to be especially made like the espagnole locks for the French doors, the handles for two internal doors, book cases, and kitchen shelves. The bookcases and shelving presented no problem as we knew a former Berliner who had all the German obsessions with exactitude that we approved of. Even the two handles proved obtainable (eventually) from a local dagga-crazed blacksmith with a flair for design but very little concept of fulfilling an order.

'Where are they Nathaniel?' Jill would hiss into the telephone after two weeks of excuses.

'Like, hey, man, it's cool, you'll get them, sister.'

'When Nathaniel?'

'Like, I've got to prioritise, sister. Say, how about Monday? Sharp, sharp.'

Monday would come and go. On Tuesday Jill would phone.

'Where are they Nathaniel?'

'Like, hey, sister, it's cool man, you'll get them.'

'When Nathaniel?'

'Ja, sharp. Sharp, sister. Friday for sure. Fully.'

Friday would come and go. And so it went on for week after week after week until six weeks had stacked themselves into Jill's temper.

'Where are they Nathaniel?'

'Hey, sister, stay cool. Like they're almost ...'

'Do you know what happened to Edward the Second, Nathaniel?'

'Hey, sister ...'

'What happened to Edward the Second, Nathaniel, was these two guys took a red hot poker, similar to one of those you've got at your forge, and they stuck it up ...'

'Like no ways, sister. That's wicked, man. Wicked.'

'You're right, Nathaniel, it's wicked. Now where are my handles?'

She got them, as it happened, not long after the story about Edward the Second.

Initially the espagnole locks seemed to be a demand too outrageous for local lock shops. Most had never heard of them and found the idea completely novel. Those who were slightly better travelled had experienced them in Europe but couldn't imagine such locks applying to Cape Town lifestyles. Those who had contacts in Europe could import them but only at exorbitant prices. We were dispirited. And then, while looking through an interior decor magazine that gave prominent photographic display to some wine estate manor Jill noticed that the French doors had espagnole locks. She phoned the editor who gave her the architect's number who gave her the number of Tobie Openshaw, a seventy-four year-old who made them in his garage workshop. Only problem he lived in Paarl, a hundred kilometres away. Jill, however, didn't see distance as an obstacle.

'Look on it as a day in the winelands,' she instructed. 'We can order the locks, do some wine tasting, have lunch on one of the estates, dawdle back in the afternoon.'

Which was how the day unfolded.

Tobie Openshaw, it turned out, wasn't only making espagnole locks in his small, well-ordered garage for the local landed gentry but also for German industrialists and Scottish lairds.

'They tell me there's nobody doing this sort of work in Europe anymore,' he remarked nonchalantly during the course of our conversation.

'One day this German businessman comes here because he'd seen the locks I'd made for some of the wine estates, and he tells me this wonderful story of how he inherited a house in England from an unknown branch of the family but that the will stipulates that he must live in the house. So he goes to England and is shown this huge house that is really in need of a lot of work. He decides to live there even though he's never lived in England before but now he's got to get the house fixed up. He needed something like two hundred espagnole locks. Let alone ordinary locks that have to be restored, or rebuilt completely. He tells me he can't find anyone in Europe to do the work, so will I do it. What could I say but of course. He paid for the shipment, everything. And an hour after I faxed to tell him the locks were ready, he had the payment transferred into my bank account.

'Another time this Scotsman comes round and says he wants me to make some locks for his hunting lodge. He's out here doing a bit of sightseeing and he visited the Castle and was impressed by the door locks. It was just fortunate for me that I recently finished remaking all those heavy locks as part of the Castle's refurbishment. So I've now got locks up in the Scottish highlands somewhere.'

Tobie had been a graphic designer most of his life and a part-time furniture maker. Some twenty-five years ago, at the request of a winemaker friend, he rebuilt a cellar door lock and the course of his life changed.

'I'd never worked with metal before and I didn't know anything about locks. But if you put your mind to it, you'll be surprised what you can do,' he offered as a homily that I've never found applicable in my life. 'Quite honestly, now I realise it was just as well things turned out the way they did. With all my shifting from company to company during my working days I hadn't kept a pension. Retiring was completely out of the question.'

The thing about Tobie Openshaw that was completely at odds with every person we dealt with during the building programme – bar the Berlin joiner – was that he delivered on time. Unlike Nathaniel the dagga-crazed smithy, unlike the builder, the window and door makers, the electrician, the plumber, the tiler, the painter, Tobie phoned two days before the deadline to say he was ready.

The espagnole locks along with door locks, toilets, basins, pedestals, door handles, shower fittings, assorted taps, tiles, and light fittings began to collect in our front room. Every day seemed to bring new requirements that we hadn't thought of: neck bolts for the shutters, trolleys for bathrooms that were to be Spartanly clear of cupboards, towel rails, toilet roll holders, chrome poles for the shower curtains, the list went on and on. The stock pile got larger and larger. This process of acquisition I found daunting. Was it necessary to have so much simply to get our house – our lives – to work? The answer each time I stepped into a hardware store was clearly, yes.

On a number of occasions, we left baskets of brass garden taps and hosepipe fittings among the shelves of hardware stores and fled empty handed, suddenly overwhelmed by the whole impossible task of putting the house together. Of course reality had to be faced eventually and usually by the next day renewed resolve and stronger nerves got us through the ordeal.

In one of these 'fleeings' I forgot on the floor of a hardware store a seal skull in a green plastic packet. The skull was a house-warming present from friends who lived up the West Coast. It was a particularly good skull with most of the teeth intact and it had been given to me an hour earlier while we breakfasted at a deli in a suburban shopping mall. But in the hardware store, flustered by the demands of neck bolts, we had bolted sans skull. And only many hours later did I notice the loss. I immediately phoned the hardware store.

'I left a green plastic bag with a seal skull in it among the neck bolts this morning,' I explained.

'Yes, we sell sealer,' came the response.

'No,' I replied, 'I don't want any sealant. I want my seal skull.'

'We've got sealer for bathrooms and for external uses. There's even one for car windows which is very effective.'

'This is a seal skull in a green plastic packet.'

'We've got sealers in white and clear, but nothing in green, I'm afraid.'

'No, no this is a seal skull. You know those black mammals that swim off our coast and catch fish. Well, one of those. Except it's not one of those it's the skull of one of those. A seal skull.'

'I'm sorry, sir, is this a new brand?'

'No, it's a packet I left this morning. A green packet.'

'Oh, you forgot something?'

'Yes, among the neck bolts. A green packet.'

'The one with a skull in it?'

'That's it. Could you keep it for me I'll be in to collect it first thing in the morning.'

'No problem.'

The next morning I arrived shortly after opening time and asked the black assistant at the till for my package. He gazed at me with a frown.

'You're white!' he said.

I nodded, not sure whether I should take his response as an accusation or a genuine display of surprise.

'Awh,' he shook his head, laughing as he handed me the plastic bag. 'A white muti man.'

17: The Bywoners

Five months before we moved out of Muizenberg a nearby cottage was let to new tenants. The previous tenants were a quiet, considerate, elderly couple who'd lived there for five years. In their stead came the original neighbours from hell. On the day they arrived there was no mistaking what bad news they would be: they revved their cars, they swore, they shouted, they played loud music, and that afternoon they drank brandy and coke on the pavement. 'Now everybody will know we're a party family,' shouted the mother, toasting the street in general.

The cottage they moved into was small: two front bedrooms, each big enough for a double bed and little else; a sitting room that could intimately accommodate at most six chairs, a third bedroom that was also a walk-through to the bathroom and toilet. A small kitchen (without hot water on tap) was off the sitting room and led to a narrow courtyard that would always be filled with washing. In here lived six adults, a teenager, a pre-teen, two small boys, occasionally a mentally-handicapped youngster, in the last months a youth installed himself, and from time to time a short bald man would appear for a few days, and then, as mysteriously, disappear.

The six adults consisted of the matriarch – a woman in her late forties – who worked at a security company; a rotund florid man who may or may not have been her partner, also in the security business; a thin man with a deformed face who was probably the matriarch's elder brother but served as the family skivvy and 'cared' for the baby boys; a young thin man, presumably the matriarch's son (yet another security officer); a masculine young woman (his sister and the mother of the two boys); a short, stocky, thuggish youth of nineteen or twenty who had no identifiable occupation. His features less closely resembled the others but he was probably the matriarch's third child. The teenager was a wild and sharp-tongued girl who kept erratic school attendance, as did the cricket-obsessed pre-teen. The two little boys ran naked, being treated more like pets from a sub-species than children.

This family was white and Afrikaans speaking. Within a few days they were referred to as Verwoerd's Bywoners, and the name stuck. Bywoners have a long tradition that goes back through the centuries of colonial settlement: essentially bywoners were poor whites living as sharecroppers or working on farms in return for accommodation and payment that was often given in kind. When grand apartheid was the landlord they benefited from his patronage but those days were now over and they had to make good in a world that offered them no freebies, no special favours, no quarter. Guile, aggression, and brazen effrontery kept this bywoner family from destitution, even helped them acquire some material possessions, but it also kept them trapped in a desperate way of life where no alternative could be imagined.

To ease this desperation they had a huge television, three stereo systems that would sometimes belt out different music at the same time, and a top-range computer with CD ROM and speakers used solely for playing games of Patience. There was no shortage of clothing, booze, cigarettes, or food. They ran two cars and two cell phones. Their front door stood open during the day and an endless stream of people visited, sometimes for hours, sometimes for a few minutes. Within days of arriving the bywoners became a social magnet in the street, always ready for a party, indeed the masculine woman jived constantly to a music that, thankfully, for the most part only she could hear. She also enjoyed karaoke, although her voice let her down. But when the brandy was in their veins, she would sing and they would dance in that tiny sitting room, and the mother's raucous cackle would reach into the depths of our house.

To be honest I was fascinated by them. They soon colonised the street, they had to, the house was too small so the street became an extension of their living area. At the slightest eruption outside I would come running from elsewhere in the house to see what was going on. I would neglect my work to watch them. I found them irresistible, a constant theatre of incident.

Firstly there was the colour issue. The bywoners immediately established relationships in the street with two dreadful coloured families – the one family ran a shebeen, the other, like the bywoners, was given to noise and street living. Despite years of apartheid the bywoners had no obvious racial prejudice. The short bald man who came and went was coloured, as was the youth who installed himself. Many of their visitors were coloured. Race wasn't the issue, class was. We ignored them, our long-standing neighbours ignored them, so they sought out the new arrivals who were part of the reason for Muizenberg's decline. In this they were repeating old patterns. As the historian, Hermann Giliomee, had commented on the urbanisation of Afrikaners in the 1930s, the tendency among some was to form friendships with coloured people. 'Many of the poorer Afrikaners found themselves in mixed slums where they struggled to sup-

129

port themselves,' he wrote. 'They could count on little active support from the better-off section of the white community. H G Luttig, a Nationalist MP, remarked in 1936 that as the poor whites moved to the towns and cities the wealthier whites ignored or shunned them. "The consequence," Luttig continued, "is that the coloured section takes notice of them and the eventual result is that the white girl or the white young man marries a coloured person."' As I stared through the blinds at the street theatre I watched this process being played out again.

The stocky nineteen-year-old couldn't keep his hands off one of the teenage girls from the corner. She was pretty with rich dark hair which he stroked at every opportunity, just as he patted her bum or brushed against her breasts. The sharp-tongued teenager acquired a coloured boyfriend. The muscular mother of the baby boys started a lesbian relationship with a coloured teenager who was put into the bywoners' care by a welfare officer. The two made no effort to keep their gropings secret. The teenager pawed at her lover in the street: draped around her, fondled her breasts, touched her crotch. Nor was the teenager a novice at sexual exploitation. She openly teased men passing in the street by sidling up to them, thrusting out her hips, partly unzipping her jeans, mouth slightly open, her tongue running over her lips. In this she was encouraged by the bywoners – especially her new-found love – as if it were a game. But quite where the game ended and prostitution began I couldn't exactly pinpoint although the street talk was wild with allegations. They were running a brothel, they were soliciting in the park, their men were no better than pimps.

I don't know. If they were whoring they weren't doing it at home, although we wondered if the regular visits of a coloured traffic cop took in more than idle family chatter over coffee and biscuits. His attentions appeared to be devoted to the sharp-tongued teenager. I once heard the muscular woman declare as she jived into the night: 'I'm going to find a man,' and the matriarch, one brandied Saturday evening, howled out: 'Ek is 'n vyf-rand-naai' to a group of black men standing in the street. There were other signs I couldn't interpret: gestures between the female bywoners and passing men, a provocation that also involved incoherent repetitions of sex-based swear words. None of this made any sense except that the encounters seemed charged with sexual overtones.

In the overcrowded world of the bywoners noise wasn't an issue. They could sleep through anything. And they couldn't understand that their loud thumping music was an intrusion on their neighbours' privacy. In fact noise was one of the major ways they established and maintained their territory. And simply by virtue of their numbers they generated a lot of noise. They talked loudly, they shouted to friends up and down the street. The baby boys whined, the cricketer bounced a ball on his bat at seven o'clock of a Sunday morning tap, tap, tap, tap. Car engines screamed, CD systems blasted, and from time to time the security officer banged and scraped at makeshift panel beating jobs.

On the first Saturday after their arrival our morning was shattered by loud music while a car was being fixed. I went outside and asked them to turn down the music. The young men stared at me for a long while and I imagined it was the kind of stare that would glaze their eyes before they beat someone senseless. Then without a word they switched off the music. I went back indoors, not triumphant at a victory but realising I was dealing with medievals, people with a very different code of behaviour. They might have complied this time but I was unsure what would happen next time. I was intimidated. I decided that unless the provocation was extreme we wouldn't get involved.

When the next incident occurred I watched my elderly neighbour go round to reason with them and felt cowardly at not rallying to his assistance.

I heard the matriarch scream at him: who did he think he was to stop them enjoying themselves? He never complained when the Angolans on the corner got out of hand. He only picked on them. They could make as much noise as they liked, for as long as they liked. Not once did she stop to listen to his complaint, or apologise for disturbing him. Instead she went straight into the attack.

On the next occasion they got out of hand we complained to their landlady but she was unconcerned. Two weeks later, driven to distraction by the constant music and drunkenness, I called the police. They subdued the bywoners, yet the following Saturday evening, the matriarch, drunk again, attacked our front door. We were reading when suddenly she started banging at the door. We raced down the passage and went outside to find the matriarch being subdued and taken away by her large partner. The rest of the bywoners stared at us from their stoep. They were braaing sausages. 'Don't worry,' the fat man joked, 'she hasn't taken her medication.' But we did worry. Mostly we worried how we were going to last through the remaining months until our house was built.

In the sixteen years I lived in Muizenberg I had to call the police out half a dozen times. Three of those calls were in the last six months and they had to do with the bywoners. The last time was at three o'clock one Friday morning in November. We were woken by loud music. The bywoners had their door closed but the lights were on and the house rocked. The matriarch's cackle came rattling above the thumping. We wondered what to do. I wasn't going to confront them but we couldn't ignore this and go back to sleep. We called the police. Five minutes later the bywoners exploded on to the stoep. Now frustrated and angry, we both went out to remonstrate with them. They paid us no heed and we retreated saying we would call the police. The cops duly arrived and through the blinds we watched the ensuing fracas as the matriarch stood hands on hips in the doorway, swearing and shouting at the constables.

'Who are you?' she screamed. 'You're not the police from Muizenberg. I know the police from Muizenberg. So why don't you come with your casspirs and lock us up?'

She pushed at the cop. He swore at her and pushed her back. Why didn't he arrest her? But no, the slanging match and the pushing and shoving continued. The two policemen retreated to their van. The thug-like youth tried to square up to them. Then, enraged, he shook his fist at our house and shouted: 'You must watch out. Pasop. I'll get you. You wit naaiers.' The police drove away. The thug continued his litany against our house. 'Where's a stone? Pasop! Watch out! You wit naaiers.' He was restrained and the bywoners trooped inside, laughing that they had bested the cops. The street resumed its quiet but Jill and I went back to bed with real concerns about what retribution would follow.

As it happened there was no sequel. For the bywoners it was just another incident, nothing out of the ordinary. We might be trembling with trepidation but to them a confrontation with the police meant nothing and even the thuggish youth had forgotten his threats. The more I thought about the incident the more it clarified the violence of the bywoners' lives. Their response to challenge was instant aggression. For them the world was a wild place and the only way to survive in it was to fight everything. Also, although they were white, they understood that skin colour no longer gave them the edge in this battle. There was a certain irony in their lack of prejudice for they understood the politics of race and expressed it eloquently. That the thug had called me a 'wit naaier' meant he interpreted white in class terms, and identified himself with an underclass that in this instance was coloured.

It was, in many respects, a matter of them against the world. Certainly I marvelled that in such a crowded household there should be no infighting. Only once did the 'skivvy' break down and rail against the family. But he was drunk and despite threatening to leave, the next day he was fetching and carrying as usual. His was the only outburst I witnessed, and although the baby boys were verbally abused and frequently smacked, the family lived in remarkable harmony.

Their language was violent, but so debased that the words no longer carried meaning. Instead they were ugly guttural detonations of sound. One of the most frequently used words was 'poes'. The baby boys were both called poes, only the tone indicating when the term was endearing and when it was censorious. Similarly 'poes' could as easily be an exclamation of pleasure as an outburst of anger. The masculine woman in particular was adept at communicating using two words 'fok' and 'poes' in 'sentences' where the pauses between the words supplied the meaning. So, trying to dissuade one of the boys from eating bubble gum he had pulled off the pavement, she said: 'Fok poes poes. Poes. Poes. Fokpoes.' Loosely translated into a middle-class mum's language this could be rendered as: 'Poofy, darling, dirty. No. No. Awful.'

18: *No Safe Havens*

Apart from the arrival of the bywoners two incidents occurred during our last months in Muizenberg that I couldn't put out of my mind. They concerned moments of violence. What troubled me were not only the residual images these incidents left, but how I reacted. I sensed a loss of influence, an admittance of social impotence, and with it a diminishing of compassion for those up against the blunt edge of life. At the same time I realised that Glencairn was not going to be the safe haven I'd imagined. There were no safe havens. Living in Cape Town meant grasping the paradox of a beautiful city writhing with violence and pain and hurt. I might be moving off the mean streets but I was of Cape Town, and being of Cape Town I had to have a hard shell.

The first incident occurred at five o'clock one spring morning. I was woken by a keening that went on and on until I realised the sad lament had been infiltrating my sleep for some time. I went outside to find a crowd had gathered three houses down, at the end of the road. They were lit by the red pulsing of a fire-engine light and blue flashes from a police van. A policeman with a weak torch beamed it up at a young man crouched on the roof of a double-storey boarding-house. The man rocked there, sounding over and over again his mantra of despair. Someone brought out a double mattress and laid it on the ground and the crowd whooped with laughter. Perhaps they were enticing him to jump.

I watched as he perched there against the parapet, his arms round his knees, his strange endless complaint drifting over the roofs bringing out more and more people. Commuters heading for the station pushed through the crowd and paused to look up at the man on the roof, and then hurried on, shaking their heads or flapping their arms in imitation of birds. They laughed and joked as they came past me.

By now firemen were raising a ladder. They got it half-way up the wall. The doleful threnody continued. Someone started speaking through a loud-hailer in a powerful voice that boomed around the streets. He seemed to call the man Jo-Jo. The firemen raised the ladder further. The crowd went quiet. The ladder wavered then banged against the roof parapet. The man stood up and jumped. He fell feet first, the length of him going down the side of the building. Then came the noise an egg makes when it rolls off a counter and smashes on the floor. And as if choreographed, as if acting out some strange ballet, the crowd sighed and swayed back and turned again to where the man must surely lie crumpled.

I saw the man falling, I heard the liquid smack of his impact. I could still see the image and hear the sound. At the moment of its happening I covered my face with my hands and closed my eyes in horror. Five minutes later the ambulance had taken the body away and I went back to bed. More significantly I went to sleep.

Days later I found out from the émigrés that the man was an Angolan. I was offered this information as if it explained his behaviour. He had no friends here I was told. Maybe he had no family. Maybe it was the war in his country. Maybe it was his head, and the men advancing these curt explanations tapped their temples. Maybe. Maybe. Maybe. No one knew for sure. No one knew how he'd got onto the roof or why he'd jumped or what his dirge had been about. No one knew where he'd been buried, or even who to tell that he'd died. As I talked to the group of men warming themselves in the spring sun it seemed there was no residue of sadness, merely an acceptance. They stood around discussing soccer and women or tinkered with their cars and the fact that recently someone had jumped to his death from the roof behind us seemed of little consequence. Maybe considering where they came from, and considering the tragic stories that so often made up their lives, one more death was simply one more death.

Here, I thought, was the point where my values came up against the reality of a Hobbesian world where life was often poor, nasty, brutish, and short. I remembered conditions at Site C where Maxwell Flekisi lived, and the gangland of Manenberg that I'd been shown by Mariette Williams and I realised that moving to Glencairn could not be seen as an escape. It might make living in Cape Town easier but there was no way of ignoring the other side of the Siamese city.

The second incident served to emphasise this point. It occurred on a warm day with a huge blue sky and the mountains in sharp definition. I went to Kommetjie – a small sheltered bay where some lobster boats are moored and children paddle around in canoes – simply to sit on a bench that overlooked this tranquillity. Before me the sea slid among the rocks giving off the pungent smell of seaweed that was so typical of the west coast. On a kelp bed sacred ibis stalked after lice and small crabs, cormorants hung out their wings in the sun, and gulls and terns wheeled overhead. I spent an hour there absorbed in the warmth and the beauty and the peacefulness.

Among the rocks and dried seaweed next to the bench lay an empty screw-top wine bottle and another one that had been smashed. Beside these was a jersey damp from the night's dew. Next to this a pale brown skirt darkly stained with blood. Not much imagination was needed to reconstruct a version of whatever had happened here: a man (or men) and a woman, drink and violence. Before I sat down I stood staring at the garments wondering if this scenario had played out the previous night, or earlier in the week and what had happened to the woman? Was she assaulted? Was she raped? Had she been able to flee? The clothing could have belonged to a shop assistant, a bank clerk, a student. Then I sighed, except for these brief moments of conjecture (which was as close as I could get to an expression of compassion) there seemed so little I could do about this. And what, ultimately, was the point of trying to envisage the circumstances? I sat down and turned my attention to the birds and the beauty of the day. Yet the presence of the skirt was always at the corner of my eye.

Of course, I could have reported the bloodied clothes to the police. But in a city with a statistical ten murders a day and two rapes a minute and an understaffed police force what would they do about a damp pile of clothes on the sand, albeit stained with blood? My imagined reconstruction led me to the words of a highway patrol policeman, Sergeant Ncamile Mase, as he recounted the extraordinary levels of violence he experienced in his day to day routine:

'One time on night shift we saw a big truck standing in the bushes. There was a man on top of the truck and another standing next to it. We drove up and spoke to them and they said, no problem they were just having some beers and enjoying themselves. The next thing I heard the one on the truck say in Xhosa to the other one that he must get us to go. So I jumped out and pulled my gun and when I looked in the back of the truck there was another man raping a girl. This girl was raped by all three of them. The way she told me her story she was walking home in Guguletu township when they stopped next to her and asked her if there was a place they could buy beers. She said she could show them a place nearby. Then she got in the truck and they went straight to the bush and raped her. This girl was stupid. You mustn't go with people at night. You mustn't go with people at any time.

'Let me tell you another thing, if you get some guys who go to a shebeen and they sit there drinking and then one asks another for a cigarette and this man says no, then it is possible he may get killed for saying no. For such a small thing. Even if a man knocks his drink against his friend's knee he can be killed for such a small thing. It's terrible. And these guys are all friends. I would say the murdering is because of drink, or a grudge, or maybe a girl. There's no respect any more. No respect.

'I'm eighteen years in the police force but these things that are happening now, these murders and rapes, there are so many. They used to happen before but much less, the big difference now is that there are so many. It's everywhere. I would say there is a devil going through the people. We in the police are fighting a big war now.'

In Sergeant Mase's accounts of the casual violence he dealt with daily were further indications of a society in trauma. Trauma that was rooted in a malaise, a listlessness, a depression that reached back into the city's colonial history. A trauma that in different ways was part of our lives in Cape Town. This was what it meant to live in Cape Town, anywhere in Cape Town.

19: Suburban Anxieties

In mid-November our soon-to-be neighbour in Glencairn decided to exact his revenge by building a three metre high retaining wall topped with a metre tall wooden fence along a short section of our common boundary. In all fairness he was simply reclaiming a corner of his land that he'd never bothered to fence because of the slope.

But now he was doing it in such a way as to block out our view down the valley. From our kitchen we'd have a view of sky and his imposing wall. More to the point he'd create a wind-tunnel between our properties which would be very unpleasant during the summer gales. There was nothing we could do about it. He was within his rights, we simply had to shrug and make the best of it. We talked about eventually covering the wall with ivy, positioning trees strategically, fastening our washing-line to it, perhaps even slinging a hammock between it and our house.

Once the wall's foundations were laid we realised he wasn't building according to plan. The plan showed the wall cut back from the corner to accommodate a planter which would have softened the structure and allowed us some view down the valley.

But as we'd already found out, plans could be changed. We decided not to object. He was so upset by our house – when the roof went on the builder had heard him cursing – that the best policy was clearly to let things be. I even offered him the use of fill from our site.

He was standing watching his workmen one morning while I searched for a sewerage connection point with our plumber. We hadn't spoken since June and he saw me approaching and looked uneasy but didn't move away. Perhaps he thought I was coming to complain about his wall. That's what I hoped. Instead I said, 'That's a helluva space you're going to have to fill up. Please feel free to use whatever builder's rubble that's lying around our site. There's also a small sand dune in the front you could help yourself to.'

'OK,' he said, adding unnecessarily, 'I'm going to need a lot of fill.'

'Well, take as much as you need,' I responded.

In the end, and predictably, he chose to truck in rubble and sand. The next time I saw his wall it was finished and the hole filled.

A day later, still on the trail of our elusive sewerage connection point at the bottom of the property, I looked up and for a moment couldn't believe what I saw. Or rather, didn't see. Where his wall had been was a huge sand dune.

My first thought was: why has he covered the wall with sand. Then I noticed his labourers were carting away bricks.

'What happened?' I shouted up to them.

'The wall burst,' one said, and laughed as if he'd never known anything this funny before.

'When?'

'A few hours ago.'

The neighbour, I later learnt, had walked beneath the wall moments before it burst and was lucky to have escaped unhurt. So were the men working on our house, let alone the plumber who had been laying pipes in the shadow of the wall earlier in the morning.

From the municipality's building department I discovered that the footings hadn't been approved by an inspector as they should have been, the wall wasn't buttressed, it had no steel reinforcing, in short it was a cheap shoddy job that had simply fulfilled its destiny. A work stoppage was placed on the neighbour's activities. His pile of rubble, however, lay on our boundary and perhaps he took some pleasure in the unsightly mess he'd made of that corner of our property.

But I had other concerns: namely, a sewerage connection point. More specifically, the absence of a sewerage connection point. According to the town planning scheme our plot was serviced, in other words it had such a point and the exact whereabouts of this elusive point was shown on a map. X in good old pirate fashion was supposed to mark the spot, but just as buried treasure was rarely found, so the plumber's digging went equally unrewarded. I called in the municipal officials responsible for drains and sanitation. We gathered at the offending corner and stood toeing the ground as if this strange ritual and our collective concentration would cause the source to be revealed.

The municipal official said things like: 'It's here on the plan, so it must be here.' Or: 'Of course there are no guarantees, sometimes these connections aren't where they're supposed to be.'

This seemed to be one of those instances. He shook his head, all the time smiling brightly, and said I was out of luck.

'But as a last resort we'll send down a probe and see what that comes up with.'

When I peered down the manhole into the dimness of the pipe I could see exactly what it was going to come up with.

'The theory is,' he explained, 'that we push the probe along the pipe. Should it encounter a hole its wheels will angle into the opening. We then measure how far it's gone and go and dig.'

Simple enough. Of course, the probe came up with nothing but what I'd expected. I didn't envy the official who had to clean it.

'What now?' I asked the municipal official.

'I'm afraid we'll have to put one in for you and that's going to cost somewhat over three thousand rand.'

'But this is a serviced plot,' I spluttered. 'Ever since it was proclaimed it's been rated as a serviced plot. It was sold to me as a serviced plot, how can you now make me pay for a connection?'

The municipal official shrugged. 'We find this happens occasionally,' he said. 'But I can't help you. You'll have to go higher up.'

I went higher up. A sympathetic female official explained to me that her hands were tied. If I wanted to be part of the flushing world I simply had to pay.

'But it's a serviced plot,' I protested. 'According to your plan.'

She grimaced to express her good intentions.

'You see,' she said, 'the municipality takes the developer on good faith. We can't go round checking every single connection point, so if the developer says he's done them, we take his word for it.'

'You're there to protect the public,' I argued. 'We pay rates so that we won't be ripped off by unscrupulous developers.'

Her voice was still kind but a little firmer now.

'Management decided it couldn't be held responsible for these sorts of problems,' she said. 'You can write to the director but I can tell you we've already had twelve cases this year and in each one the people had to pay.'

'You're telling me I have no recourse.'

She nodded. 'You could sue the person who sold you the plot.'

True, but somehow that didn't seem fair. At stake was a larger issue: a well-known property developer had laid out and serviced the housing estate and sold plots on this basis. The more I thought about it, the more I felt they had a moral obligation to make good. That the development had been completed a quarter of a century earlier didn't really affect the situation to my way of thinking. In a city where history was a constant reckoner an omission twenty-five years ago remained an omission today.

By the time I got home – minus three thousand three hundred rand, a factor that truly rankled – I had composed a fax.

To Old Mutual Properties: 18 November 1999
Dear Sir
In 1998 I bought a plot in Glencairn Heights. Before and after buying I ascertained from the South Peninsula Municipality that the plot was serviced and was shown the various connection points on the council plan.

I have subsequently built on the site. Two days ago, despite extensive searching by my plumber and the municipality's drainage department, the sewerage connection point could not be located. I have now had to pay R3300.00 to the municipality for this connection point to be installed.

As Old Mutual Properties was the developer of Glencairn Heights – and as a plan of the sewerage lines prepared by your contractors, Ninham Shand, clearly shows a sewerage connection point on my property – I feel your company is responsible for the omission, and should reimburse me. The municipality confirms that Old Mutual Properties certified that the sites were serviced and it was on this basis that they were originally sold and rated.

I believe that I am not alone in experiencing this problem in Glencairn Heights.
Yours faithfully

To Old Mutual Properties: 23 November 1999
Dear Sir
On 18 November 1999 I faxed through the following letter. To date I have not had any acknowledgement of receipt let alone a response. This matter is now extremely urgent and your immediate reply is anticipated.

From Old Mutual Properties: 23 November 1999
Dear Sir/Madam
Your fax dated 18 November 1999 refers.

We have requested information from Ninham Shand regarding the services to the site. This documentation is in deep storage and will take some time to retrieve. We will in due course revert to you in this regard.

Could you please in the interim forward details of the site to us. Yours faithfully

To Old Mutual Properties: 23 November 1999
Dear Sir
Thank you for your response to my fax of 18 November.

While I appreciate that your subcontractors, Ninham Shand, will have to resort to their archives, I can assure you that an original Ninham Shand plan detailing the sewerage connections in Glencairn Heights (which I have seen) is still being used by the South Peninsula Municipality. This can be viewed at the offices of the sanitation department.
Yours faithfully

From Ninham Shand: 25 November 1999
We acknowledge receipt of your faxes dated 18 and 23 November in this regard.

We have recalled our files and can confirm the following: In 1971 we were appointed by Old Mutual Properties to prepare the plans and tender documentation and administer the contract for the services of Glencairn Heights No 5. The contractor who installed these services, including the main sewers and connection points was Messrs Clifford Harris (Pty) Ltd.

Kindly inform us of the area in which the search for the connection was undertaken and to what depth, as after all these years it could be 1–1,5 metres underground. Also indicate where the concrete was finally made.
Yours faithfully

To Ninham Shand: 25 November 1999
Dear Sir
My plumber tried to locate the connection point as per the Ninham Shand plan where it is shown as being in the southeast corner of the

property approximately one metre from that boundary peg. He dug down to the sewerage pipe which was about a metre below the ground and then uncovered 1–1.5 metres of the pipe within my property and about a metre into the adjoining property. When this search failed to locate the connection point he called in the municipality's sanitation department who inserted a probe but failed to find a connection point.

I trust this will help resolve the issue.

Yours faithfully

To Old Mutual Properties and a copy to Ninham Shand: 1 December 1999

Dear Sir

It is now virtually two weeks since I first wrote to Old Mutual Properties about the missing sewerage connection point at my property. I have subsequently supplied you and Ninham Shand with the names and telephone numbers of the plumber and municipal official who could confirm this. According to a fax from Ninham Shand received on 25 November 1999 they confirmed being appointed by Old Mutual Properties to prepare the plans and to administer the contract for the services of Glencairn Heights. The contractor who installed these services was Messrs Clifford Harris (Pty) Ltd. The issue seems to me to be relatively simple: something that should have been there was not installed.

I do not appreciate having the matter dragged on in this manner. Nor do I appreciate not being kept informed of what progress is being made towards resolving the issue. Consequently I would ask you please to settle the issue today.

Yours faithfully

From Ninham Shand: 1 December 1999

We have provided information to Old Mutual Properties regarding the original contract and would suggest that in future you direct all communications in this regard to their office.

Yours faithfully

A phone call from Old Mutual Properties assured me that they would inspect the site during the next few days and get back to me as soon as possible.

From Old Mutual Properties: 7 December 1999
Dear Sir
We have established that the contractor who originally serviced the development no longer exists. I will be forwarding your claim to our executive committee for their consideration. Could you please forward to this office proof of payment of the amount claimed.
Yours faithfully

To Old Mutual Properties: 7 December 1999
Dear Sir
Attached is a copy of the receipt for the R3300.00 I paid to the South Peninsula Municipality to have the connection point inserted. This work was carried out on 23 November 1999.
I trust this will help your executive committee resolve the matter.
Yours faithfully

From Old Mutual Properties: 9 December 1999
Dear Sir
Further to our recent correspondence and telephone conversation, we have established that the original contractor who serviced Glencairn Extension 5, Clifford Harris (Pty) Ltd no longer exists.
On advice from our legal counsel, we do not believe that you have any claim against Old Mutual Properties (Pty) Ltd, in contract or in delict. We further believe that the prescription period for this work has expired.
As a gesture of goodwill, and without any acceptance of liability on the part of Old Mutual, our Executive has agreed to pay you an *ex gratia* amount of R3300.00.
Please find attached our cheque in the above amount.
Yours faithfully.

20: The Nine Circles Of Hell

It all started with the plumber – a special kind of hell reserved for those audacious enough, or foolish enough, to build a house. Up to late October, I'd thought the project was a cakewalk. The walls were up, the roof trusses were on, the carpenter was about to fit the tongue and groove ceiling, the electrician was about to do the wiring. Completion date was two months away, the rainy season over, clear skies ahead. We'd proved our friends wrong: 'You'll end up in a bun-fight with the builder,' they cautioned. 'It happens to everyone.' Yet we had experienced no problems at all. This was a stress-free, hassle-free project. We were about to take a week's holiday and there didn't seem to be any reason why we couldn't. We'd walked through the house plug point by plug point with the electrician; we'd shown the plumber exactly where taps, basins, toilets, showers had to be positioned and he'd quaintly spray-painted our requirements on to the walls.

'Take your holiday,' said the builder confidently. 'Everything's in hand.'

This was our first time off since the trip to Rügen Island in 1997. Before us stretched a week at De Hoop nature reserve: whales off the beach, an endlessly fascinating birdlife, ghostly eland rubbing against the cottage at night, books, magazines, quiet. On a Friday afternoon, two days before we were due to leave, the plumber sent a fax detailing the items he would need the next week. I stared at it in disbelief. Why now? Why had he waited until the last moment? While much of what he wanted was stacked in the front room, much, like the hot water cylinder, stop cocks, drip trays, breaker valves, hard water elements, undreamed of traps and hoses still had to be purchased. Nor was this a one-stop expedition: to get the best deal we had to buy all over the city. There was nothing for it but to cancel the holiday. Instead we devoted the week to shopping for plumbing. And started on a pathway into hell. As we descended ever deeper matters went increasingly awry and the devils became ever more malicious.

By the time we reached the Inferno's First Circle, Enoch, the electrician's mate, wielding an angle-grinder with gay abandon, had cut channelling into bagged-brick walls that would not be plastered. After carefully positioning light points on double-skin walls, and impressing on the electrician that before any cuts were made we were to be consulted, the walls of our dream house now resembled a Berlin apartment after a scary night in 1944.

At the Second Circle stood Chris, the impish plumber, who wouldn't install sanitary ware or the hot water cylinder or any of the oddments we'd sacrificed our holiday to acquire until the week before we moved in. With a wave he watched us descend to the Third Circle where Abdullah waited patiently. Abdullah had been contracted by the builder to lay white cement floors in the main bedroom and the study. These floors Jill had devoted considerable energy to researching. They were to be a feature of the house. White cement had to come from Portugal. Sand had to come from Malmesbury. A special bonding liquid was required in a recipe that was as exact as it was difficult to come by. More importantly, considerable skill was called for by the artisan. A metal float had to be wielded in small circular movements drawing the water to the surface of the screed for a marble-like finish. Abdullah shrugged in disdain at our instructions. 'I know this work,' he said.

Of course when the ingredients were required there was no white cement to be had in Cape Town. Our move-in date was three weeks away. What now? we asked the builder. Fear not, he replied, a shipment was due soon. Thus began a saga of the high seas: the ship had encountered heavy weather, one of the ship's engines had failed. The ship would dock tomorrow. No, it was only expected the following afternoon. The engine had been repaired, the ship would make port during the night. Two days later the freighter sailed in. The saga continued ashore: the white cement had been unloaded and would be at the depot by midday. At four o'clock it was thought the white cement had been hijacked by swimming pool companies. At five o'clock the white cement arrived. On a weekend two weeks before the contract deadline, Abdullah set to and made a passable job.

Except that lurking in the dark corners of Circle Four were Leslie, the painter, who liberally splashed paint onto the pristine surface, and the glaziers who trod in putty, and Charles, the electrician, who imprinted his boot soles in the wet sealer. None of these marks could be erased. Our floors were spoilt.

At Circle Five was Nimrod, a gofer, who dropped a chemical on to a section of the study floor which meant the entire floor had to be broken out and re-laid three days before the deadline. By now Abdullah was in no mood for fine finishes so he made large and lavish passes with the float over the screed and his handiwork dried to the pattern of a beach at low tide. In a final gesture of goodwill he blocked a shower outlet with a plug of screed that set as hard as granite and would give me many happy hours over Christmas chopping it out. But this was hell and my groans were merely part of a general chorus.

Abdullah stood back for us to pass on to Mohammed, the grinning tiler at Circle Six. His speciality was laying just enough tiles to lure us into thinking the floors would be finished the next day. But the next day Mohammed would not appear. He taunted us in this way until the day before we moved in when he finally laid the last slate tile.

Circle Seven was the preserve of the carpenter, Dean, who promptly broke an espagnole lock, hung shutters upside down, drilled screws through rebates, hinged doors randomly, and, many many weeks later would make our deck without pride or pause. In fact I would consider keeping fish in some of the holes he'd drilled to countersink the screws.

But if these devilish guides to the upper circles were specialists in torture they were nothing compared with the princes awaiting us in the depths. For down on Circle Eight, rubbing his hands with glee, was Mark from the company that had made the windows and doors and shutters. He produced a front door that was warped (which the builder had to replace with a door from another company), and then supplied warped windows and warped French doors and warped shutters. Every time I opened his half-finished sash windows I risked a hernia rupture and could hear him chortling in the sulphurous depths.

And then, of course, on Circle Nine was Graham the builder himself, finally revealed as the Lucifer we had been warned about. He was still the perfect gentleman who listened to our grievances and agreed and sympathised, but for the most part he actually did nothing. On 20 November I made a list of the work still to be completed: French doors needed to be hung; locks fitted; fireplace floor screeded, landing constructed, wiring finished in the bedroom and hall; white cement floors screeded, walls patched up, sanitary ware fitted, bathrooms painted, internal walls painted, under-floor heating laid, windows glazed, garage door installed, light fittings installed, deck and pergola constructed, retaining wall built, drive way laid, house painted outside, tiling done, sewerage connected, electricity connected, porch floor completed, cladding fitted, site cleared. By 17 December, the contract deadline, that list was only slightly diminished. There were walls that needed to be patched up, the garage door was yet to be installed, the drive way was non-existent, the house hadn't been painted outside, there were no tiles in the stairwell and kitchen, the deck and pergolas remained details on the plan, the porch floor was a rough slab of concrete, the cladding lingered as an unrealised building challenge, and the electricity inspector hadn't blessed our house with power. We delayed our move to the following Monday and then again to the Thursday before Christmas. Even as the movers packed our furniture I was in Glencairn watching the electricity inspector connect us. I wasn't entirely confident there would be light but more by a miracle than our electrician's expertise, there was. I entered our new house where one toilet out of three worked and one shower out of two. Four windows lacked shutters, the other shutters couldn't be opened because there were no shutter hooks to fasten them. We couldn't see the view and there would be no New Year drinks on the deck simply because there was no deck.

'I had so hoped it wouldn't be like this,' said Jill wistfully.

One year later: for the record I need to tell how (and when) the building project ended. I also need to state that Jill's lament – 'I had so hoped it wouldn't be like this' – became a refrain we uttered many times during our first year in the house when bad-mouthing our builder's handiwork and inefficiency. Within a few days it became clear that the three sets of French doors and their shutters on to the yet-to-be-built deck were of inferior quality and warped. The same applied to a window in the bedroom and another in the study. We decided to reject them and have them replaced. And although there were problems with almost all the other windows and the sliding door hung at an angle we reluctantly agreed to retain these at a reduced price.

Piqued by our demands, the doors and windows contractor eventually walked away from the job saying he had no intention of replacing the disputed items and leaving one of our sash windows in pieces with the lead weights lying on the floor. It would take nine months before the builder had the window fixed let alone the French doors replaced. That was November 2000. During the next three months two sets of replacement shutters had to be returned (in the one instance they were too short; in the other not wide enough) before shutters were fitted to these doors but even then they were incorrectly styled. With our patience now exhausted we sighed and said we'd keep this, the fourth set, provided the price was reduced. The builder looked miffed. I felt he should have been thankful he wasn't talking to our lawyers.

Because in those fourteen months it had taken the builders two months to construct the deck and a further six months before the hand rail was installed and strung with nautical wire. In the middle of winter water seeped into the foundations spreading damp up one of the study walls and across the floor. During the repair work it was discovered that a buttressing section of the foundations had been left incomplete with no concrete reinforcement. Although this oversight was hastily corrected the damp continued and three weeks later the builders were back to redo the waterproofing with more care and attention. In the process they destroyed plants and left garden steps at strange and dangerous angles. There were other minor irritations: the winter rains poured through the ill-fitting sliding door, starlings invaded the ceiling because the builders had neglected to put in the vermin proofing stipulated in the plans, we discovered that the hot water pipes were of a material called Polycop when they should have been copper and went round the outside of the house when shorter routes should have been taken through the house, and in a final spurt to finish painting shutters and windows that had been left untouched for the better part of a year, paint was splashed on a newly-bought roman blind, ruining the material. Correcting these problems took time and always involved disruptions. In fact it seemed that over the fourteen months there wasn't a week when we weren't dealing with the builders: either inconvenienced by their presence or arguing over the quality of the work or what remained to be done.

Eventually in the middle of February 2001 we asked them to send a final account. There were windows, doors and shutters where the painting was still unfinished but neither of us could face another day with the painter and his random brush. Nor did we wish to have anything more to do with the builder.

21: On The Wind-Blown Peninsula

More than a year has passed and the constant noise of the social issues that made Muizenberg compelling but an impossible place to live are memories. Whereas daily life there was determined by people – the voices of those rushing to catch early morning trains, followed by children heading for school, the mid-morning vegetable sellers, the postman, the fighting of the afternoon drunks – in Glencairn the pattern could not be more different. It is set by birds, the colour of the sea, the shift of the sun about the house, the screech of cicadas.

We wake to the piping of francolins picking through the garden and the squabbling of guinea fowl in the firebreak. During the day the birdsong is from prinias, bulbuls, bokmakieries, and the high-pitched twittering of sunbirds. Late most afternoons a southern bou bou raucously dodges through the bushes after insects and in the evening four white-backed ravens come down the valley swooping over the roofs, heading for their roost in the quarry. The birds define the seasons too for in spring I often woke at night to nightjars calling across the mountain. By summer they were gone but then a pair of steppe buzzards perched on the black trees (the ghosts of the Storkwinkel tree) that I can see through the study window.

Each morning at breakfast we gaze enthralled over False Bay, having learnt to tell how the day will unfold by the blueness of the early morning sea. Last winter we watched long strings of cormorants pass low over the water and huge shoals of yellowtail stream across the bay in a frenzy. There have been schools of dolphins, and, of course, the whales.

Ironically the first whale we saw one dim July morning was dead. It floated into Glencairn bay at first light and washed up on the beach. I went down to watch the police divers secure ropes around the carcass and haul it back out to sea for the sharks to feed on. The smell was powerful. Pedro Fernandez's whale came to mind, not exactly a sense of déjà vu but a feeling that something hadn't changed.

Two months later whale sightings were a daily occurrence. At any hour a cursory glance at the bay would reveal a glistening back, the fountain of a 'blow', a black tail about to slip beneath the surface, or a whale leaping across the middle distance. For three months the bay was thick with life, and then, suddenly, the whales were gone.

Over the months we have become attuned to these changes and to the moment-by-moment changes in the weather: a shift in the wind, or the start of a cold front passing over in ridges of cirrus, or a thickening of the horizon haze in summer which usually heralds a southeaster.

The southeaster is a phenomenon we have been forced to take into our lives. Although we have lived with this wind for twenty years and know that it can topple buses and snatch off roofs, the narrow streets of Muizenberg were remarkably protected. The wind went over the top of the houses.

For our first few days in Glencairn the southeaster was down and then one afternoon a breeze went to gale force in a matter of hours. Being half way up a mountain, facing south east there was nothing to protect us. Hour after hour for five days the wind banged against the house. It screeched under the doors and through the rebates, it rattled in the ceiling. Gripped with anxiety I lay awake for most of the gale's first night imagining that at any moment the roof would be torn away. The wind was not a constant blast: what made it so frightening were pockets of stillness that could last as long as a minute. Suddenly the rushing noise would stop. Ordinary sounds would return: a dog barking across the valley, a distant car accelerating, the hum of the fridge. As the silence lengthened the tension became unbearable. When would it strike? Perhaps it was dying down? Then came a thrashing as the wind struck into the trees and barrelled up the valley until it boomed against our house. My chest would constrict, my heart thump; sometimes I buried my head beneath the pillow. After three days our nerves were raw. We began to wonder if we had made a dreadful mistake. We heard of people who had been defeated by the southeaster and retreated to the older suburbs where the wind was not a psychological condition. We were also told that we'd get used to it. So we bought ear plugs and set about accepting that at least half of the summer would be at gale force. If once I had been picked out for joking about living on a wind-blown peninsula, the joke was now on me.

But after another season of southeasters we have become acclimatised: not used to it, rather hardened against it. The wind still frays our nerves and after three days of a blow I can sense a tightening of the skin at my temples and a brittleness in our conversation. We are far out to sea on a roaring trade wind. We listen to the house, to its creaking and thumping the way sailors must have listened to the timber and rigging of their ships as they rounded the Cape. We listen with some dread, but know there will be calm days to come.

Afterword: 'It's A Beautiful City Don't Mess It'

In mid-June 2000 I revisited Berlin. I had to go back. Now that we had changed our lives I felt a compulsion to see how Berlin's grand attempt at reinvention had progressed.

That weekend was the annual carnival and all through a hot Sunday with temperatures in the upper twenties, float after noisy float of painted figures threaded through the streets of Kreuzberg. I'd seen it in 1996, again in 1997, and I dragged a reluctant Thomas to Mehringdamm so that I could see it again.

Not that I liked carnivals but I wanted to watch the Berliners having fun. Thomas hated it.

'This type of activity is for my nephews and nieces,' he protested. 'They like this kind of nonsense.'

Thomas had not been before and could see no reason to go now. Long ago, in the days of the Wall, he had chosen to live in Berlin and had a fierce passion for the city, but the carnival was not part of how he understood Berlin.

'Be careful of your wallet. Watch for pick-pockets,' he warned me as we pressed through the crowds. Yet he indulged my whim, and once I'd had my fill of the sweat and beer throngs, we fled to the quiet of a pavement café on Oranienburgerstrasse for coffee and Kuchen.

One of the reasons I wanted to re-experience the festival was because Cape Town's art galleries had open nights in the city centre and I'd found in these an expression of the city's sense of fun. People danced in the streets, talked on corners, sat on the curbs to eat street food. The cafés were full, the hordes pressed up and down the pavements, laughing, joking, enjoying themselves. In effect, reclaiming a city that had fallen silent at night because no one lived there anymore.

On one of these occasions as I leaned against a wall watching the dancers I noticed black men in dark suits and dark glasses moving through the crowds. They were wired and would occasionally turn their heads into their lapels and speak into hidden microphones. I started looking for the cabinet minister whose goons they must surely be, then noticed, somewhat to my consternation, that one was angling towards me. I'd thought I was invisible against the wall. Maybe he had other ideas. In the suit, shades and wires he was ominous. Unsmiling. Even when he handed me a strip of paper I still believed he was for real. The message on the paper read: 'Let us enjoy our childhood. It's a beautiful city don't mess it.' He smiled and slid away into the crowd to dish out more of his sentimental but touching idea.

What happened at the annual Berlin carnival and the Cape Town 'art nights' was a celebration of a city, of a sense of place. Even while they were demonstrations against the excesses of history, the festivals attempted, if only for a moment, to give their respective cities a vibrant present. As imperfect as that gesture might be, it spoke of people who liked living where they were.

Not that Thomas saw it this way. 'These are just ... how do you say it? ... hooligans,' he said between mouthfuls of cheese cake.

I disagreed, but then when it came to the new Berlin, he and I disagreed about many things.

For instance, the new buildings on Potsdamer Platz were thrilling. The shapes, the textures, the walls of glass, the sheer audacity of this monument to reinvention gave me goose pimples as I walked along the broad pavements, already well-spotted with chewing gum. I marvelled at the architectural imaginations that had turned the desolate, spooky no-man's land on the eastern side of the Wall into what could become a vibrant downtown. Even if the buildings had put too much office space on the market too quickly they worked for me simply as statements of aspiration. Maybe something of my enthusiasm was tied up with the building of my own house. I had come to look on the physical act of building as renewal and creation: the most explicit demonstration of faith in the meaning of a place that one could make. Berlin had re-imagined itself with considerable audacity, an audacity that Cape Town lacked because mostly (the Waterfront being an exception) this energy to imagine the city was dissipated into shopping malls.

However, Thomas hated the buildings of Potsdamer Platz. He regarded them as an attempt to make Berlin something it was not, to turn this section of his city into a poor version of Manhattan. He felt the buildings would remain empty monoliths to the egos of internationally acclaimed architects who should never have been let loose on such an historic site.

He was not alone in this sentiment. In Stresemannstrasse, on a three metre section of the Wall that had been retained as a memorial, a group against any further eradication of this chapter of the city's history had painted three panels depicting the breaching of the Wall on 9 November 1989. Beneath the pictures were the words: 'Don't Destroy History'. In 1997 I had felt the same. But now that so many of the buildings were finished it was difficult not to be impressed by the way in which the city was renewing itself. Nor did I think the buildings obliterated history. The memorial saw to that, but so did the Berliners because they constantly remembered.

For instance, one night in 1997, returning late from a reading at Café Einstein, I was waiting at a bus stop on Nollendorfplatz with Thomas. This was the district where Christopher Isherwood stayed from 1929 to 1933 living the material that would go into *Mr Norris Changes Trains* and *Goodbye to Berlin*. I knew this and half expected Sally Bowles to come gliding with nineteen thirties panache through the comic-book tits-and-arse whores who worked these streets. What I hadn't anticipated was Thomas's question: 'Do you know what happened where we are standing?'

I shook my head.

'Here the Nazis brought all the gays from Nollendorf before taking them to the concentration camps.'

In that instant what had been an innocent bus stop became a place of frightened people, most of whom were going to die. These corners abounded in Berlin, they were what made the city uncomfortable. And no amount of building was going to erase this sort of memory. As long as people remembered, the city wouldn't lose its soul. So while the ghosts that Thomas conjured up were painful reminders of a city become the heart of fascism, his act of remembering confronted the city's shame. Nothing was redeemed or absolved, but nothing was forgotten. This seemed to me important in the life of a city.

Some years ago I had a similar experience in Cape Town. I was to interview an Anglican priest, Michael Weeder, one of the leaders of a coloured organisation called the December 1st Movement, and we had agreed to meet on the traffic island in Spin Street where a round concrete memorial stated in English and Afrikaans: 'On this spot stood the old slave tree.' This seemed appropriate as the December 1st Movement commemorated the date Britain's Emancipation Decree was enacted in the Cape Colony. And now, for the first time in more than a hundred and sixty years, the shame that had kept the heritage of slavery suppressed was being pushed aside. The group wanted to recognise the suffering of their forebears while emphasising the skills, culture, and effort that an enslaved society had put into developing the city.

While I waited in the midst of the morning traffic a businessman crossed the street: he was wearing a dark suit, white shirt, a discreet red striped tie and well-polished black shoes. He carried a briefcase and had a cell-phone clipped to his belt. He was a man of his time. This was his city, he walked confidently through its streets.

'Excuse me,' I said pointing at the memorial which gave no dates or reason for its significance, 'can you tell me what this means?'

He read the inscription aloud. It was the first time he'd noticed it.

'I don't know,' he said. 'Maybe there used to be slaves here a thousand years ago. Maybe it's something historical like that.'

He laughed, wanting to get away, baffled by my question.

'I don't know,' he said again. 'I can't help you. It's something to do with slaves.'

I watched the businessman hurrying away towards the Groote Kerk. I watched until he turned the corner into Adderley Street. He was coloured. It was likely some of his forebears were sold on this spot. It was likely some of his forebears spent their years in the adjacent Slave Lodge.

As the inscription said, a tree grew on that spot. It became known as the slave tree because in its shade people were auctioned once a week.

A few minutes later Michael Weeder arrived. He looked like an Anglican priest should. He was solidly build, his face round and friendly. His eyes were a sympathetic brown. He was wearing leather sandals.

He looked down at the inscription. 'What does this say?' he asked rhetorically. 'What does this tell you about what happened here? Families were destroyed here. Children sold to one person, their mothers sold to another. A woman sold to a farmer in Stellenbosch, her man sold to a merchant in Cape Town. Can you imagine that? Can you just imagine what it was like, all the misery that happened here on the ground beneath our feet.'

He looked away down the street as if he could see slaves waiting to go on auction.

'This is a sad place,' he said.

Then he told me a childhood memory: it was about his mother who would always say a prayer whenever she passed near this spot. When he asked her why she did this he was told that bad things had happened there to 'our people'. But what the bad things were he didn't find out until much later.

'This doesn't acknowledge what was done to our people,' he said placing his foot on the memorial. 'There is no sense of spirit here, no sense of the past. This is not a place where you can reflect on the suffering of those people. If you can't see the country's past, if you can't hear the voices from the past then you can't understand the present.'

The search for a sense of place in a city is also a search for that place where the city is most itself. For me this is Greenmarket Square. Centuries ago this was a vegetable market and a meeting place. In the evenings, slaves would gather outside the Town House 'in such numbers as to fill a great part of the square', noted a contemporary observer. He also called it the slaves' 'place of resort.' It must have been a noisy, friendly, raucous time. These days, after years of sterility, that time has returned. On the steps of the elegant building are Zimbabweans selling soapstone carvings, Nigerians selling West African masks, and on the stoep tourists drinking coffee. It has become a meeting place again. So has the market in the Square. Among the clutter of stalls and pressing bodies, the bartering and good humour is an older market filled with vegetable hawkers and country traders, men in top hats and tails, wagons, carts, horses, oxen, dogs. In this market, depicted in the drawings of Charles D'Oyly in 1832, the languages were probably as diverse and loud as they are today. In one of his pictures the mountain rises behind Town House and the buildings that enclose the square in a warm embrace. I can stand where he stood, see the Town House he saw. I can imagine, then as now, disappearing into the market jostle, becoming part of the city.